ACLS History E-Book Project

Reprint Series

The ACLS History E-Book Project (www.historyebook.org) collaborates with constituent societies of the American Council of Learned Societies, publishers, librarians and historians to create an electronic collection of works of high quality in the field of history. This volume is produced from digital images created for the Project by the Scholarly Publishing Office and the Digital Library Production Service at the University of Michigan, Ann Arbor. The digital reformatting process results in an electronic version of the text that can be both accessed online and used to create new print copies. This book and hundreds of others are available online in the History E-Book Project through subscription.

Many of the works in the History E-Book Project are available in print and can be ordered either directly from their publishers or as part of this series. For information refer to the online Title Record page for each book. Inquiries regarding this series can be directed to info@hebook.org.

ACLS

HISTORY E-BOOK

http://www.historyebook.org

THE PARMA ILDEFONSUS
A ROMANESQUE ILLUMINATED MANUSCRIPT FROM CLUNY AND RELATED WORKS

MONOGRAPHS ON ARCHAEOLOGY AND FINE ARTS

SPONSORED BY

THE ARCHAEOLOGICAL INSTITUTE OF AMERICA AND

THE COLLEGE ART ASSOCIATION OF AMERICA

XI

THE PARMA ILDEFONSUS A ROMANESQUE ILLUMINATED MANUSCRIPT FROM CLUNY AND RELATED WORKS

BY

MEYER SCHAPIRO

1964

PUBLISHED BY THE COLLEGE ART ASSOCIATION OF AMERICA

IN CONJUNCTION WITH THE ART BULLETIN

The publication of this monograph
has been aided by a grant from the
Samuel H. Kress Foundation

✧

L.C. Card No. 64-17286

PREFACE

THE substance of this monograph was presented in a lecture at Dumbarton Oaks in April 1958. The typescript was completed at the Center for Advanced Study in the Behavioral Sciences, Stanford, in the fall of 1962. I wish to thank Mrs. Joan Warmbrunn of the Center for retyping the entire text and Professor H. W. Janson for good suggestions in editing the work. I am indebted also to the staffs of the Columbia University Libraries, the Frick Art Reference Library, the Pierpont Morgan Library, the Cabinet des Manuscrits of the Bibliothèque Nationale, Paris, and the Biblioteca Palatina, Parma, for their kind help, and to the publisher Sansoni of Florence for photographs of the Parma manuscript and to Moreno of Madrid for those of the Madrid Ildefonsus (Bibl. Nac. lat. 10087). Mr. Albert Skira has generously placed at our disposal the two colorplates, originally reproduced in André Grabar and Carl Nordenfalk, *Romanesque Painting from the Eleventh to the Thirteenth Century*, Geneva, 1958. The index was prepared with the help of Mrs. Marlene Park.

TABLE OF CONTENTS

THE PARMA ILDEFONSUS A ROMANESQUE ILLUMINATED MANUSCRIPT FROM CLUNY AND RELATED WORKS

INTRODUCTION

IN THE art of Cluny about 1100 may be distinguished two styles, a native Burgundian Romanesque and what may be called an Italo-Byzantine. Of the first, the best known examples are the capitals from the choir of the abbey church,[1] and of the second, the miniatures of the lectionary in the Bibliothèque Nationale in Paris, MS Nouv. Acq. lat. 2246 (Figs. 37-39).[2] There is also a fragmentary painting in a gradual from Cluny (Paris, Bibl. Nat. lat. 1087) in a Germanic variant of the Romanesque style (Fig. 40),[3] and another example of the Italo-Byzantine in the great frescoes in the chapel of Berzé-la-Ville (Figs. 44-48).[4]

This duality of styles about 1100 is not peculiar to Cluny.[5] In other centers in France—at Limoges, Dijon, Angers—we observe a similar practice of two styles. In the frescoes of Saint-Savin, the two styles (or at least distinct elements of these styles) occur within one work, probably by the same hand; thus, in the Offerings of Cain and Abel (Fig. 49) the brothers are drawn with the banded lines so common in the Romanesque sculptures of southern France, while God who receives Abel's gift is painted with streaks of light based on conventions of Italo-Byzantine art.[6] This example permits us to see how different meanings could be attached to the two styles as symbolic modes of expression.[7] In the Stavelot Bible (British Museum, Add. MS 28106-28107), completed in 1097, the contrast of the two styles is apparent throughout the book. Finally, in Cîteaux, we can follow the interplay of the styles in successive periods. In the earliest manuscripts, dating from the first decade of the twelfth century, only the native Romanesque style appears. Later, and especially in the 1120's, the second style is dominant.[8] This change corresponds perhaps to the new role of the order of Cîteaux under Saint Bernard, when the Cistercians replaced the Cluniacs as a leading spiritual force in the Western church.

1. See V. Terret, *La sculpture bourguignonne au XIIe et XIIIe siècles*, Cluny, Autun-Paris, 1914; A. K. Porter, *Romanesque Sculpture of the Pilgrimage Roads*, Boston, 1923, I, pp. 71-108 and ills. 5-9.

2. See Fernand Mercier, *Les primitifs français. La peinture clunysienne en Bourgogne à l'époque romane*, Paris, 1931, pp. 23-80, pls. 92-107.

3. See note 12 below.

4. Mercier, *Les primitifs français*, pls. 1-65; A. Grabar and C. Nordenfalk, *Romanesque Painting from the Eleventh to the Thirteenth Century*, Geneva, 1958, pp. 103-109, with colorplates.

5. This duality of styles is not the same phenomenon as the coexistence of the Mozarabic and Romanesque in Spain or the Anglo-Saxon and Norman in England about 1100, which I have discussed in ART BULLETIN, XXI, 1939, pp. 314ff. and note 4. In those examples it is a matter of an old native style surviving for one or two generations beside a newly introduced foreign style. In France the native Romanesque is itself a highly productive, developing art.

6. Note also that Cain, unlike the other two figures, is in profile; the deviation from the usual three-quarters pose of the head expresses here by contrast a moral difference, and helps to characterize Cain like other evil, demonic, and socially inferior figures in early medieval art.

7 On the concept of "modes" as distinct from styles, perhaps applicable here, see my remarks in *Review of Religion*, VIII, New York, 1944, pp. 181ff., and E. Kitzinger, *The Mosaics of Monreale*, Palermo, 1960, pp. 20ff. An interesting parallel on a lower level of quality is a miniature in Vatican lat. 4922, the Vita Matildis by Donizo, 1114-1115 (P. Schramm, *Die deutschen Kaiser und Könige in Bildern ihrer Zeit*, I, *751-1152*, Leipzig-Berlin, 1928, fig. 113). In the scene of Henry IV kneeling before Matilda and Hugo of Cluny, the emperor is painted in the Italo-Byzantine cloisonné fold style with comb-shaped lights, the other two figures in unmodeled Romanesque forms. The Byzantine conventions apply here only to the monarch, though he is humbled (the inscription reads: "Rex rogat abbatem / Mathildim supplicat atque").

8. See C. Oursel, *La miniature du XIIe siècle à l'abbaye de Cîteaux d'après les manuscrits de la Bibliothèque de Dijon*, Dijon, 1926.

CHAPTER I

THE PARMA CODEX

THERE exists a richly illustrated manuscript from Cluny in which the Italo-Byzantine style and a Germanic variant of the native Romanesque occur together. This little-studied codex, MS 1650 in the Palatine Library of Parma (Figs. 1-36 and Colorplates),[9] contains the treatise of Ildefonsus, bishop of Toledo (ca. 607-667), on the Virginity of Mary. Its origin in Cluny is evident from several facts. The handwriting is of a kind that appears in the parts of the cartulary of Cluny (Paris, Bibl. Nat. MS Nouv. Acq. lat. 1497-1498) executed around 1100 (Fig. 66).[10] A similar handwriting is found also in the lectionary (Bibl. Nat. Nouv. Acq. lat. 2246) which came to Paris from the library of Cluny (Figs. 37-39, 57). The decorated initials (Figs. 22, 28, 30, 32-35) are of precisely the type current in manuscripts from Cluny in the late eleventh and early twelfth century (Figs. 57, 65-66), including both the cartulary and the lectionary.[11] It is a local variant of a Germanic style of spiral foliate ornament widely practiced during the period of the Ottos and their successors, in a large region extending from Eastern France and Burgundy to Southeastern Germany and to Italy—the region of the Holy Roman Empire. Of the two hands that painted the figures in the Parma manuscript, the first—which produced all but two of the thirty-five miniatures (Figs. 1-35 and Colorplate I)—belongs to the artist of whom a fragmentary trace has survived in the mutilated manuscript, Paris, Bibl. Nat. lat. 1087, already mentioned (Fig. 40). Here we find, besides, the identical style of initials and other ornament (Figs. 41, 43) that appears in the borders of the Parma Codex.[12] The second hand, which painted the two concluding miniatures in an Italo-Byzantine style (Fig. 23 and Colorplate II), is remarkably similar to the artist who produced several miniatures in the Paris lectionary (Figs. 37-39).

If the late Georg Swarzenski, an admirable scholar whose judgment must always be accorded considerable weight, thought that the miniatures of the Parma manuscript were the joint work of a Bavarian and an Italian painter, it was because of the striking resemblance of the first hand to a number of paintings in manuscripts from Regensburg and Salzburg where he had found just such a conjunction of a Germanic and a Byzantinizing style.[13] The plan of the Parma Codex, with every page of text enclosed by an elaborate frame, often by modeled ornament of acanthus and perspective meanders, and with so many pages of miniatures on gold backgrounds, and large foliate

9. I had studied this manuscript and photographed it in 1931 in connection with researches in Cluniac art. My friend, Carl Nordenfalk, whom nothing in medieval manuscripts escapes, has independently inferred its origin in Cluny; see Grabar and Nordenfalk, *Romanesque Painting*, pp. 189f.

10. On the dating of the cartulary, see pp. 59, 60 below.

11. See pp. 26ff. below.

12. Cf. Figs. 22, 28, 30, 32-35 for the initials; Colorplate I and Figs. 11, 21, 25-27 for the borders. All but one of the miniatures originally in this manuscript have been torn out. From the impressions of the missing pages on the adjoining ones, from the inscriptions, and from the spacing of the text, I conclude that there were at least nine painted miniatures and possibly ten or eleven: Nativity (between fols. 7 and 8), Magi (12-13), a pre-Passion episode (43-44, in Quadragesima), Crucifixion (55-56), Resurrection or Marys at the Tomb (56-57, two leaves torn out), Ascension (65-66), Pentecost (69-70), Annunciation to Zacharias (74-75), Unidentified (75-76), Peter in Prison (on a stub of fol. 75 bis—there was perhaps also a scene of the Martyrdom of Peter and Paul), Unidentified (two leaves torn out between fols. 110 and 111—possibly the Martyrdom of St. Vincent). The manuscript was written in the last quarter of the 11th century by the same hand as the rubrics and majuscules of the Parma Codex—cf. Figs. 22 and 41. An office in honor of St. Odilo was added on fol. 112v at the beginning of the 12th century. See Dom Hesbert, "Les témoins manuscrits du culte de Saint Odilon," *À Cluny, Congrès Scientifique. Fêtes et cérémonies liturgiques en l'honneur des saints Abbés Odon et Odilon, 9-11 Juillet 1949*. Travaux du Congrès, Arts, Histoire et Liturgie, publiés par la Société des Amis de Cluny, Dijon, 1950, pp. 57, 92, 102ff., 119.

13. See *Die Salzburger Malerei von den ersten Anfängen bis zur Blütezeit des romanischen Stiles*, II, Leipzig, 1913, p. 83 and n. 1. He regarded the script as Italian. See also his *Regensburger Buchmalerei*, Leipzig, 1901, pls. XXIII, XXVIIIff., XXXIII, for examples of the two styles and their fusion in manuscripts of Regensburg and Salzburg (pl. XXVIII is a Salzburg manuscript painted by Bertolt, now in the Morgan Library, MS 780). The Parma Codex was called a German manuscript by Max Manitius, *Geschichte der lateinischen Literatur des Mittelalters*, I, Munich, 1911, p. 235, n. 2, and by the editors of the catalogue of the great exhibition of illuminated manuscripts held in Rome in 1954—see bibliography in note 18 below.

initials in gold and silver on a purple ground—this conception of the book as a work of art recalls the sumptuous treasure-manuscripts produced for the German rulers. Among these are several that were made for the emperor Henry II, formerly Duke of Bavaria,[14] who was also a patron of Cluny and a dear friend of the abbot Odilo.[15] The latter's successor, Hugo, maintained through the second half of the eleventh century the same close relationship with the German imperial house: he was the godfather of the emperor Henry IV. When in the Parma Codex the painter has to represent a royal figure such as David, he gives him a gabled crown of German imperial type (Fig. 8).[16]

One could suppose from the long association of Cluny with the German emperors that both the Germanic and Italo-Byzantine elements in the Parma manuscript were based on German art and especially on the south German centers which before 1100 had begun to absorb the Byzantine forms. It should be observed, however, that the Ottonian ornament does not appear in the art of Cluny until after Odilo's death in 1049 and long after the rule of Henry II (1002-1024). A Bible made for Odilo toward the end of his life (Paris, Bibl. Nat., MS lat. 15176) still shows little trace of the Ottonian style.[17] Not until the time of the abbot Hugo (1049-1109) do we find in the manuscripts of Cluny that Germanic type of initial. The book art of Cluny, relative to that of other great monastic centers in the eleventh century, seems to have been quite backward. Only toward 1100, when the great church was under construction, did Cluny produce works that were abreast of the more advanced schools. But this judgment rests in part on the scarcity of Cluniac painting; few decorated manuscripts of Cluny have survived from the period before the last quarter of the eleventh century, and its early wall painting is still unknown.

The Parma Codex has therefore a special interest, apart from its high quality, as evidence of the otherwise scarce manuscript art of the greatest monastic center in Western Europe at a moment of intense stirring in art, when monumental stone sculpture was revived in Burgundy and in the Cluniac order at large and a new architecture was created.

14. Cf. the sacramentary in Munich, lat. MS 4456 (Swarzenski, *Regensburger Buchmalerei*, pls. VII-IX, and A. Goldschmidt, *German Illumination*, New York, 1928, II, pls. 72, 73); Vatican, Ottob. lat. 74, Gospels of Henry II (Swarzenski, *ibid.*, pls. XIX-XXI; Goldschmidt, *ibid.*, pl. 78); Bamberg), Staatl. Bibl. 95 (A.II.46), from Seeon (Goldschmidt, *ibid.*, pl. 79).

15. See Jotsaldus, "Vita Odilonis," Migne, *Pat. lat.*, CXLII, cols. 902, 904; for the friendship of Hugo with Henry III, see Hildebertus, "Vita Hugonis," *ibid.*, 159, col. 864.

16. For the German examples, see page 23 and note 70 below.

17. I plan to publish a study of this manuscript in the near future.

CHAPTER II

DESCRIPTION OF THE PARMA CODEX[18]

THE Parma Codex consists of 111 parchment leaves with text and illustrations, 23 cm. by 16 cm., between two blank leaves in front and a blank leaf at the end. The three unused leaves are without numbers in the modern pagination, but the first two (fols. i, ii) seem to belong to the same gathering (of eight) as fols. 1 to 6, and the final leaf forms a union with fol. 111.

On every full page of text are nineteen long lines of writing between pencil rulings. The script is a regular minuscule of about 1100, stable and distinct, without slope, and with a beginning of fracture in the growing contrast of thick and thin strokes and the analysis of the round letter into these separate elements (Figs. 29, 7-24, Colorplate II). The middle zone predominates, the upper and lower are perfectly balanced. There are few ligatures beside the usual & and st. Another hand, less advanced in style, has written the rubrics and most of the inscriptions in rustic and Roman capitals.

The text, framed throughout by bands of gold and silver and an occasional purple, and most often with painted foliate and geometric motifs between the gold and silver bands, is enclosed in a space of 145 mm. by 85 mm. The outermost border is 185 mm. by 125 (to 127) mm. These dimensions will give an idea of the small scale and preciousness of the book. It is wonderfully preserved; the text and illuminations are intact. Only the last page, folio 111, suggests an accident (Fig. 36). It was written later in a script that imitates the original hand, and seems to replace a page that was removed or lost.[19]

Of the thirty-five miniatures, nine are full-page; thirteen are half-page or slightly more (Figs. 7-10, 12-17, 20), and three are one-third of a page or smaller (Figs. 11, 18, 19); the remaining ten are bust portraits of prophets, about an inch or two square (Figs. 18, 19, 29).

This variety in the format of the pictures, which were newly designed illustrations rather than copies—a variety that required of the scribe and the painter an effort of thought in adapting text and pictures to each other for the first time—has some interest for the history of book art. It points to the complexity of design possible in the scriptorium of Cluny at this time, a complexity which we would not surmise from other manuscripts, although it is consistent with the character of the new church building.[20]

18. BIBLIOGRAPHY: Paolo Paciaudi, *Ad codicem membranaceum saeculo X. exscriptum quo liber B. Hildephonsi episcopi Toletani Peri Trion Apiston continetur.* Parma, Biblioteca Palatina, MS 1589, vol. IV, 23 pages (ca. 1761-1771), a description and analysis of the manuscript and its illustrations; idem, *Il bibliotecario diretto nel formare, classare e continuare una publica biblioteca* (Vincenza, 1785), 4th ed., Rome, 1863, p. 51, on the value and historical importance of the Parma Codex for its script and paintings; A. L. Millin, *Voyage dans le Milanais,* Paris, 1817, II, p. 122, n. 3, on the library of Parma ("on y remarque, parmi les manuscrits, . . . le Traité de saint Ildephonse, De Virginitate beatae Virginis, avec des miniatures singulières"); Federico Odorici, "Memorie storiche della Nazionale Biblioteca di Parma," *Atti e Memorie della R. Deputazione di storia patria per le provincie Modenesi e Parmensi* (serie Ia), Modena, III, 1867, pp. 425ff.; *Atlante Paleografico-artistico* per cura di F. Carta, C. Cipolla, e C. Frati, Turin, 1899, pp. 19, 20 and pl. XXI (fols. 9v, 10—Ildefonsus kneeling before the Virgin, and initial D); Max Manitius, *Geschichte der lateinischen Literatur des Mittelalters,* Munich, 1911, I, p. 235, n. 2; Georg Swarzenski, *Die Salzburger Malerei,* Leipzig, 1913, p. 83; A. Boselli in *Tesori delle biblioteche d'Italia,* I, *Emilia e Romagna* a cura del Prof. D. Fava, Milano, 1932, p. 210, and fig. 89 on p. 208 (reproducing fol. 4; he dates the manuscript in the 10th century, like Paciaudi and Odorici, and the editors of the *Atlante Paleografico*); *Mostra storica nazionale della miniatura,* Palazzo di Venezia, Roma, *Catalogo,* Firenze, 1954, p. 108, no. 150, "probably Bavarian"; Carl Nordenfalk, in *Romanesque Painting from the Eleventh to the Thirteenth Century* (*Mural Painting* by André Grabar; *Book Illumination* by Carl Nordenfalk), Geneva, 1958, pp. 189, 190, with reproductions in color of fols. 4v, 5, 102v. Dr. Nordenfalk plans to publish an article about the manuscript in *Art de France,* 1964.

19. I neglected to examine the structure of the gatherings of the whole manuscript. Most of the quire numbers have been cut by the binder; they survive on the lower margins of fols. 46v (VI), 54v (VII), 70v (VIIII), in the hand of the original scribe.

20. As in the latter, the greatest concentration of imagery is at the head (fols. IV-45v)—cf. the chevet; there follows a long section of text (fols. 46-101v) with ornamented frames but without pictures, like the nave; and finally, towards the end (fols. 102, 102v) are the twin miniatures of the colophon, like the decoration of a façade.

Nine large ornamented initials with interlacing spiral foliage (Figs. 22, 28, 30, 32-35) introduce the major divisions of the text. These letters, together with the incipits and opening words written in gold majuscules, are set on a purple ground and are paired with a full-page miniature on the adjoining page (Figs. 5, 28). One of the initials (fol. 5) shows Ildefonsus praying to Christ; the scene is painted in the same style as the preceding miniature on fol. 4v (both on Colorplate I).

Like the choice of initials, the subjects of the miniatures correspond to the divisions and content of the text. The main work, Ildefonsus' treatise on the Virginity of Mary against the Infidels and Jews, in six chapters or *lectiones*,[21] is preceded by a eulogy of the author by Julian, a later bishop of Toledo;[22] it is followed by a lengthy colophon borrowed from a copy of Ildefonsus' work executed in Spain in 951 by the monk Gómez for Gotiscalc, bishop of Le Puy.[23] After this colophon comes a life of Ildefonsus by Cixila, here mistakenly attributed to a Spaniard, Elladius.[24] This colophon was so important to the sponsor of the Parma Codex that he had it illustrated by two original pictures (Fig. 23 and Colorplate II) representing the scribe and the recipient of the copy made in 951. The latter, which is now preserved in the Paris Bibliothèque Nationale (MS lat. 2855), has no illustrations at all.[25]

21. It is not the whole of the treatise, but ends abruptly, like Paris, B.N. lat. 2855, the ancestor of the text of the Parma manuscript. See page 62 below. For this text see Vicente Blanco García, *San Ildefonso, De Virginitate Beatae Mariae. Historia de su tradición manuscrita, texto y comentario gramatical y estilístico*, Madrid, 1937, and Migne, *Pat. lat.*, XCVI, cols. 53ff.

22. Migne, *Pat. lat.*, cols. 43, 44.

23. L. Delisle, *Le Cabinet des Manuscrits de la Bibliothèque Nationale*, Paris, 1868-1881, I, p. 516; Blanco García, *San Ildefonso*, pp. 11ff., 53ff. See also note 268 below.

24. Migne, *Pat. lat.*, XCVI, cols. 43-47. I must ask the reader's indulgence for the inconsistent forms of the proper names. I have used modern forms where they are in common use and otherwise the medieval Latin forms.

25. It is described in detail and collated by Blanco García, *San Ildefonso*, pp. 11ff., 53ff.

1. *Ildefonsus writing*, fol. 4v; *Ildefonsus praying*, initial D, fol. 5, Parma, Bibl. Palatina, MS lat. 1650, ca. 1100

CHAPTER III

THE CHOICE OF SCENES

THE text of Ildefonsus is a theological work, an impassioned tirade against the silent heretics and unbelievers—Jovinianus, Helvidius and the Jews—who do not admit (among other things) that Mary was perpetually virgin and that she was the mother of God. One can imagine a number of scenes from the Gospels pertinent to this theme—like the Infancy cycle that is so common in medieval art. The text of Ildefonsus, however, lends itself to a wider range of illustration, for in the course of his argument Ildefonsus refers to many figures and episodes of the two Testaments, like the Crucifixion, the Resurrection, the Ascension, Jonah and the Whale, the Three Children in the Furnace, etc. In a Spanish manuscript of the same treatise (Florence, Laurentian Library, Ashburnham MS 17), written in Toledo in 1067, there are numerous miniatures representing events from the life of Christ, to which there is only a passing allusion in the text.[26] In the Parma Codex the artist has kept closer to the writer's polemical line. Not the theological concepts themselves are represented or symbolized but the religious authorities who are named in the text. The prophets and patriarchs of the Old Testament cited by Ildefonsus as predicting the advent of Christ are painted in twenty-two frames. In nine of these pictures they are shown addressing the Jews (Figs. 7-11, 14, 17, 19). This argumentative content also underlies the five scenes that represent Ildefonsus debating with his opponents (Figs. 4-6, 13, 20). Beside these images of the protagonists in the theological dispute, there are two scenes of Ildefonsus praying to Christ (Colorplate I and Fig. 21) and six scenes of solemn aspect: Ildefonsus at the altar, at his desk writing the book, and kneeling before the Virgin (Figs. 2, 3, and Colorplate I); a picture of the bishop Julian (Fig. 1), the author of the life of Ildefonsus that precedes the book; and last, the already mentioned pictures of Gómez writing the copy of Ildefonsus' work in 951 and presenting it to the bishop Gotiscalc (Fig. 23 and Colorplate II). Surprising in a book that glorifies the Virgin is her subordinate place among the illustrations: she appears in only one of the thirty-five pictures (Fig. 3).

In this exceptional choice of subjects as well as in the treatment, we recognize the influence of a monastic milieu where religious observance and orthodoxy are the main interests. These are indeed important, even central, features of spiritual life in Cluny towards 1100. Many of the accompanying figures in the paintings are represented in Cluniac dress and tonsure, and Ildefonsus himself, though a bishop, is represented in monk's habit.

The significance of the choice of subjects will become still clearer if we compare the manuscript with older illustrated theological texts. What emerges then as distinctive in the Ildefonsus Codex is the large place given to the author himself. He is shown not only in the act of writing, but as a leader in the religious community; he writes surrounded by monks; he teaches, argues, and celebrates mass. The model here is not the life of Christ and the saints as illustrated in the gospel manuscripts and hagiographical pictures of the preceding period. For if certain compositions in the Parma Codex might have been adapted from older images of Christ and the saints, none of the miracles attributed to Ildefonsus by his two biographers in the same manuscript are represented. The scenes chosen have a contemporary flavor and are perhaps inspired by the living examples of the great abbots and reformers of the eleventh century, especially in the Cluniac order.

The text and the subject of each miniature are described more fully in Appendix I. I shall go on to the style of the paintings and ornament, beginning with those by the first hand.

26. The manuscript is described by L. Delisle, *Notice sur des manuscrits du Fonds Libri conservés à la Laurentienne, à Florence*, Paris, 1886, pp. 23, 24, and by Blanco García, *San Ildefonso*, pp. 16, 17, 48, 49 (MS F).

CHAPTER IV

THE ILDEFONSUS PAINTER (HAND A)

THIS hand, which I shall call A and sometimes "the Ildefonsus painter," works with opaque pigment over a pen drawing of thin red lines. These are disclosed in Fig. 15, where the painting has flaked. (In Paris, Bibl. Nat. MS lat. 1087, fol. 28, a little bust in an initial Q is rendered by a similar pen drawing in red.) The lines of contours and folds—painted in a deeper tone of the local color of the object, sometimes approaching black, and in places as thick, relatively, as the leading of stained glass—make a strong rhythmical network. The figures wear light red, green, blue and purple robes; the buildings, also outlined and detailed in color, are in red, green, blue and yellow. A uniform pink flesh tone is applied to the faces and hands, with reddish patches on the cheeks and with black lines for the features.

Together with the gold ground, the colors form a scale of luminosities, like a jeweler's palette of precious stones and metals, hard and bright in the red, soft and absorbing in the deep purple, enamel smooth in the green and blue fillings of the initials.

Figures and setting cohere as a continuous colored tracery against the pure gold which shines through the open arcades and windows and even through the tiny arches of a seat—a perforate effect at all levels of the scene (Colorplate 1).

Although the technique seems to entail a flat, linear representation, there is an effort at modeling. Different devices are applied for this end, but without a consistent plan in the choice of means. There is perhaps a connection with qualities of the particular figures, those in monk's costume being treated differently from the others. In certain figures the local color of the costume is graded from light to dark in broad parallel strokes to produce an effect of mass and relief (e.g. Ildefonsus and the figure behind him on Fig. 2). The buildings, too, and especially the columns, are modeled by a gradation of at least three values of the local color. On the borders the curling of acanthus leaves and the pleating of the meander ribbons, with their decided perspective effects, are reinforced by the contrasting tones; they give to the whole painted image an appearance of the tangibly real.

Beside the suggestive rounding of the bodies through strong curved contours and girdling folds like the hoops of a barrel, fine white lines model certain of the figures and especially the monks (Figs. 3-5). Parallel and serried, in alternately vertical and horizontal sets between the dark folds, these lines are sometimes joined by a perpendicular that gives a comb-like form to the set, which is enclosed more or less completely by straight or curved strokes. On the robes of lighter color there results a faint weave of light without shadow, a fanciful ornament spun across the entire costume. It is not a true modeling so much as a decorative lighting or lightening, as if the artist wished to spiritualize the heavy envelope of the body by a delicate web of tenuous lines that evokes a finer substance within or behind the costume. White lines appear also as a real applied ornament on a figure (Helvidius in Fig. 5).

With all these devices of modeling, the weight of the forms seems to depend most often on the emphatic strength of the dark lines of the contours and the folds. The envelopment of the body by overlapping robes is another factor in suggesting volume. The artist takes pains to show the back of a tunic in the foreshortened hem at the feet.

Turning from the technique, which one can hardly describe without touching on qualities of style, let us consider the forms in themselves as structure and expression.

These are most complete in the scenes with elaborate architectural settings. Here a particular gift of the artist, a fully developed conception, stands out clearly.

CHAPTER V

THE ARCHITECTURE

BUILDINGS, represented as the interior and exterior of the space of an episode, are combined with figures that possess architectural qualities: postures and lines of the costume are often like columns, arches, towers and moldings (Figs. 1, 3, 4). The figures have the sobriety and weight of the constructed environment, a pervasive stiffness and solemnity, while the buildings have the air of an organized human group with both rigid and flexible elementary forms. The same heavy outlines, the same clear colors and mode of grouping colors in stratified sets against the common gold ground, are applied to figures and buildings alike.

This architecture is not a conventional pictorial enclosure that shapes the figures. It is both a milieu and a frame, and more effectively a milieu—a constructed open-work setting, changing from scene to scene and sharing many traits with the figures. Sometimes the figures appear to be bounded by the architecture and to conform to it in their posture, gesture and accessories (Colorplate 1 and Fig. 3); elsewhere the figures cross the architecture and seem to intertwine with it (Figs. 2, 5); but always we see them together, not as if one were added to the other, but as a single, close-knit whole, a model of men-and-buildings. The ornament of the borders, too, is often brought into expressive accord with the forms of buildings and figures through similar, easily legible shapes, colors and rhythms.

A remarkable example of this constructed unity of architecture, figures and frame is the picture of Ildefonsus writing (Colorplate 1). His cowl forms a strict horizontal spanning two columns that provides a base line for an arch, parallels and inverts a stilted lintel beside that arch, and brings into the group of figures the triangular motif of the gable. The pattern of this brilliantly conceived headdress of Ildefonsus reappears in rotation in the cowls of the monks and in parts of his own costume (the chest, the left arm and shoulder, the right leg) and even in the background void behind his head; it returns in close analogy to the gable in the repeated double V-folds of the monks. On the border the winding, half-palmette scroll transposes into curved plant forms some of the inversions, rotations and continuities of elements of the figures and buildings.

If a figure is like a column and arch, it is not because the body has been "deformed" to fit the architecture. But figure and architecture have been subjected together to an ideal of order in which qualities of both the represented figure and the building are realized. The architecture in turn centers, balances and accents an element of the human content and helps to bind or unify. Throughout the series of pictures, the buildings are limited in their range of forms, but in each scene there is another choice of architectural members.

In the page of Ildefonsus before the Virgin (Fig. 3) the lower buildings, subtly opposed to each other in direction and form, support the contrasted postures of the kneeling saint and the enthroned Virgin, and establish a balance of left and right. The structure at the Virgin's left side is rendered with marked perspective foreshortening, while the one behind Ildefonsus is broadly parallel to the picture plane. Correspondingly, the first has a domical roof, rounded like the Virgin's headdress, and the other is gabled like the saint's cowl and maintains the general angularity of his form. Because of the symmetry of the structures in the spandrels above, the oppositions of the buildings in the scene are even more pronounced and expressive; in the strong emotional context of the subject they have perhaps a latent meaning in the psychoanalytic sense.[27]

27. As I have said, it is the only miniature in the book that represents the Virgin, although the whole work of Ildefonsus is dedicated to her. She is constantly referred to in the text as a house, a mansion, an edifice ("mansionem divinitatis . . . domum divinitatis . . . omnipotens est artifex aedificii hujus," fols. 16v, 17). Odilo in a sermon on the Assumption of the Virgin (Migne, *Pat. lat.*, CXLII, col. 1028) says: "Tu es enim aula regalis . . . virgo perennis. . . ." The

The architecture is the "world" of these figures and may be regarded also as the world of the monk-painter, his own milieu projected and idealized.

Although certain elements of the architecture depend, as we shall see, on the preceding Ottonian art, it is unlike the latter in that buildings and figures in Cluny are, formally and expressively, about equal in visual weight. If in some German works the architecture is not only a frame or background but a milieu, in Cluny it is a milieu with a corporate sense like the monastery itself, a collection of buildings enclosing a group rather than a single authoritative figure. In Ottonian art, this quality of the architectural background is approached mainly in the setting for an isolated power—emperor, bishop, pope—as a sign of rank.

The buildings are tied to the frame, touching it on all four sides. Columns of the interior reach to the lower border; columns at the sides are attached to the vertical borders, and the roofs and gables to the upper frame. The knobs of roofs and gables are aligned on the inner band of the frame. The building is not an aedicula set inside the space of the picture; at no point does it break through the frame as in many medieval works.

Though arbitrary as a representation, this pictorial architecture retains the aspect of monastic buildings of the time. The numerous columns, windows, arches, roofs and gables, the vertical articulation and the many levels, transmit something of the quality of the great Romanesque churches. The complex horizon of the architecture, so typical of the Middle Ages, when the tall churches dominated the towns and villages as if the church or abbey were a city in itself, reminds us of the view of old Cluny, with its fantastic conglomeration of roofs and towers (Fig. 64).

The interiors, rendered without perspective, recreate effects of openness, airiness, and elevation and, through the bright colors and ever-present gold of the background, luminosity as well. The new spaciousness of the Romanesque church interior, formed of many sub-spaces of crypt, aisles, galleries, choir, chapels and ambulatory, on different levels and at different depths, has its equivalent in the varied levels and sizes of arches, columns and windows in the miniatures. There is even a search for perspective, very primitive and incidental, it is true, in the foreshortening and diminution of repeated elements on the gables, roofs and finials of Fig. 3. Much depth has been telescoped in these shallow represented spaces, and a great height has been evoked through the upward succession of members. I do not doubt that the artist was inspired in his architectural imagery by the buildings rising around him in Cluny and elsewhere in Burgundy. He is aware of the new flexibility of the arch and, within the same picture, draws, beside the familiar semicircular form,

miniature precedes Ildefonsus' prayer to the Virgin: "Domina mea, dominatrix mea . . ." (fol. 10) and is intended to illustrate this text. It may be influenced by the account of the Virgin's miraculous appearance to Ildefonsus in the apse of his church; she was seated on his ivory throne and offered him a gift, the famous chasuble ("accipe munusculum de manu mea quod de thesauro Filii mei tibi attuli"). The book in the Virgin's hand recalls the story of Saint Leocadia transmitting to him the Virgin's thanks for his defense of her purity. Both miracles are reported in the life of Ildefonsus by Elladius (sc. Cixila) at the end of the Parma Codex (fols. 110v, 111; see Migne, *Pat. lat.*, XCVI, cols. 47, 48).

But if the contrasted forms of the buildings in the picture correspond to the opposed male and female characteristics of the two figures, how shall one interpret the conspicuously opened door below the Virgin—who is called the *porta clausa* in medieval commentary? A few leaves beyond the picture, on fols. 16v, 17, the artist could read in Ildefonsus' reply to the unbelieving Helvidius the author's denial that anyone could approach the door of God's house, closed after his passage from it ("ne portam domus Dei, ejus exitu clausam, a quocunque posse adiri contendas . . . celorum rex est possessor iuris istius . . . omnipotens est artifex aedificii hujus. Nemo cum illo ingressus est, nemo regressus . . ."). He could read also, on fol. 28v, a paraphrase of Ezekiel 44:2, on the closed gate of the sanctuary, reserved for God alone ("domus dei cuius pudoris integerrima sunt claustra ad orientem consistens porta semper est clausa . . . qui solus ipse Dñs per eam nascendo transivit"); and on fols. 47v, 48 a further reference to the closed door of Ezekiel's text as a prophecy of Mary's purity: "item iuxta Ezechielem agit, ut de hac materni uteri domo per pudoris virginei portam idem dñs d̄s israel egrediatur . . . eadem porta sit clausa, quia semper est virginitatis vera conclusa." In the open door, has the artist projected an unconscious wish in the psychoanalytic sense? For a parallel, cf. the relief of the Doubting Thomas in the cloister of Santo Domingo de Silos, where the representation of the Doubting Thomas, with the probing of Christ's wound behind the closed doors (*fores clausas*), has evoked an imagery of sexual contrasts, including a marginal scene of a city with open doors and paired male and female musicians playing contrasted instruments (see ART BULLETIN, XXI, 1939, p. 337, fig. 17, and pp. 348, 349, n. 123, for my observations, and A. K. Porter, *Spanish Romanesque Sculpture*, Florence, N.Y., n.d. [ca. 1930], I, pl. 36). Just as the Doubting Thomas is the only one among the six early reliefs of the cloister with buildings represented on the spandrels of the arched frame, so in the Parma Codex the door of the scene with the Virgin is unique in the entire series of miniatures with architectural settings.

various stilted, depressed, segmental, and ramping arches, adapted to different, sometimes asymmetrical supports and elevations. The exceptional page of the prophet Micah addressing hearers in the city (Fig. 17) presents some well-observed details of a contemporary town.

In this architecture of the full-page scenes, the figures possess no common ground line or plane but seem suspended in the space (Colorplate 1 and Figs. 4-6). (In several pages and especially in the rendering of crowds, the lower extremities are omitted; see Fig. 6.) It is as if the painter, wishing to represent them as in the real depth of an interior, assigned them a place beyond the lower frame which rendered the foreground limits of the building, yet felt no need to bind them to a supporting floor. In other miniatures, where there is no interior setting, the painter has placed the figures directly on the lower border as a ground, or even on a band that defines a ground plane (Figs. 7, 10). The elevation of the figures in the scenes enacted inside a building is therefore a deliberate choice, an artistic device that the artist undoubtedly inherited from older art. In several scenes a floor line or plane is provided as a base for a single figure (Figs. 2, 4, 5); but this line is raised well above the lower border and is even tilted, as in a diagonal perspective view, suggesting the picturesqueness of these church interiors with the varied steps and levels of choir, transepts, aisles, and chapels.

Without the constraints of a rational perspective, the apparent relation of the figures to the buildings is clearly imaginative and beyond physical possibility, as in much of Romanesque and pre-Romanesque art. A scene is shaped as a piecemeal aggregate of the figures and of equally distinct architectural members, with much overlapping that evokes depth but without regard to a consistent and well-ordered succession of points or parallel planes in three-dimensional space. Enclosed above and below by a building in the picture plane, the figures seem to be inside the structure; but reaching horizontally from border to border and overlapping the columns in that zone, the figures also appear to be in front and therefore outside the building. On one page (Fig. 5) a figure (Helvidius) is drawn intertwined with a column, with one foot in front of, the other behind the column. (The interlace does not, of course, represent an intended intertwining of body and column; this the medieval artist was capable of rendering, however, when he wished to show Christ in the scene of the Flagellation or a possessed figure attached to a post—he conceived the intertwining then as a posture of the fettered body or as a means of expressing the inwardly entangled spirit of the victim.) Like the *en face* position of the eye in a profile Egyptian head, which was not designed to be read as a glance directed to us as observers, or like a halo in Christian art drawn behind the head, whether the head is shown in a front, back, or profile view, and always designating the same connection of the halo with the head, so certain relations of figure and column in the Parma miniatures are, in a broad sense, syntactical, not semantic, and should not be construed as representing particular positions in space, although in the context of the whole they may, as unique and sometimes strongly accented overlappings, contribute to effects of relief and depth. A parallel example that illuminates the problem is the drawing of the scepter of the Emperor Otto II in the leaf of the Registrum Gregorii in Chantilly (Fig. 68); though intertwined with objects in different planes in depth, the scepter was undoubtedly understood by the artist (and is seen by us today) as a perfectly rigid vertical in a plane parallel to the picture surface.[28] We may liken the method to a language in which the words for spatial position ("on," "in," "under," "over") are used in some contexts in a non-spatial sense ("the game is over"), or consist of phonemes that occur as parts of words without spatial significance ("over," "clover"). In the medieval paintings it would be a serious misinterpretation to regard this interlacing of forms as an intended characteristic of the *represented* space or objects.

28. In a similar way the position of the emperor *inside* the canopy is sufficiently expressed by showing his head *under* the arch of the canopy, although the rest of the body and his throne are represented as if (from the point of view of later methods of representation) outside the canopy.

CHAPTER VI

THE FIGURES

BEFORE advancing further on this line of historical comparisons, let us look at the figures by themselves. I shall take as an example those of the first painting which illustrates the bishop Julian's eulogy of Ildefonsus and shows the author and his flock (Fig. 1).

They are like the architecture not only in the rigid postures, but in the formation of the figures out of many repeated elements, some of which appear in identical shape in the building. The contours of the bodies, for example of the monk at the right, are dark heavy lines, straight and rounded, like the columns and arches; the long limbs are columnar, and the resemblance is confirmed by the ornament of the central column. The two arches are surmounted by domed towers that may be seen as a population of the spandrels. The arcade on which the figures stand is adapted to them: centered through a large middle arch under the bishop, or triple-arched to correspond to three figures at the right.

This unity of figures and buildings proceeds from another feature of the style: the construction of the whole out of a large number of distinct elements, each of which is repeated often in both figures and buildings, and is discernible, too, as a type that has a definite place in an order of elements of different size. Tiny scattered dots represent the hairs on the tonsures and beards of the men and reappear in another order, a linear set, as an ornament of the collars, and again in the domical roofs of the towers and in the meanders of the frame; a little enlarged, these dots become the pupils of eight eyes, an element of the central column, and an ornament of the black-bearded figure at the right; drawn as circles of the same size, they are strewn on the costumes to mark the axis of Julian's legs and of the first monk's torso, and grouped in threes they are a triangular ornament of the lower limbs and arms and shoes. A still larger round unit is repeated in the knobs of the nine structures above the arches in a straight line and reappears strategically in the crozier; short parallel vertical lines, like the teeth of a comb, make up the fringes of the bishop's stole; longer lines in diagonal sets of three mark the tiles of the roofs; on a somewhat larger scale are formed the folds of the monk—segments of arcs, paired and tripled, radial and concentric—clearly of the same family as the arches of the buildings that include segmental forms and asymmetries, but always in pairs or larger sets. The spiral of the crozier is a special instance of such a type, similar to the small lateral arch-and-column forms below and the intercepted windows of the towers above. The horizontal elements—astragals, imposts, bases, cornices—are examples of the same habit of ordered design; and less simple though equally classifiable are the domes, capitals, and bases with their forked and petaled ornament which reappears surprisingly in the black beard of the figure at the right. The lines of the features—brows, eyes, nose, lips—also belong to these series. I have counted no less than twenty-seven such distinct motifs of drawing in this one picture.

Between the smallest unit and the largest, which is the whole figure, there seems to be a chain of elements of increasing size, just as in the architecture there are dwarf and giant columns, small and large arches, and elements that appear in unique groups, in twos, threes and fours. More interesting—the small and large are brought into connection through obvious or hidden similarities of shape. Thus the chasuble of Julian, zigzag in form, is coupled with the beard of the figure at the right, though the pattern is inverted; and, more ingeniously and mysteriously, the odd ornament of the central column, like a corked bottle, suggests a human form in rigid vertical succession, but also a third element of analogy in the triad of figure, tower, and column. A discreet variation in this file of ornament gives us a sample of the painter's inventive humor: in line with the knees of the two main figures, the "bottle" becomes circular and is marked with a center—a unique accent that rhymes with the eye-like pattern of the knees of the right figure.

One will notice, too, that the strongly modeled meander of the frame in its stiff, right-angled turns has a vague yet compelling analogy to the scene that it encloses. The basic T-shaped unit with stepped returning lines is an angular version of the large form uniting the two arches and the columns with the upper contours of the two main figures, whose extended arms touch the central column. The meander ribbon carries around the border in a rigid sequence the theme of symmetrical contact and enclosure in these figures.

Fascinating in its formal rightness and expressive power is the crozier, strictly vertical and with rounded and pointed ends. On another page (Fig. 4), the same crozier is suspended in a doorway with artful choice; the rounded handle is set against the rectangular stilted lintel, the enlarged pointed tip is between columnar bases that frame and accent its sharpened thrust which reverses the line of the gable above the doorway. It is one of three gables with a reinforced zigzag pattern rhyming with the forked beard of the same antagonist. The meander border, angular and pointed, distributes the motif of the crozier's point around the entire field.

These subtleties keep us from describing the repeated elementary forms as a primitive, reductive style, the devices of an artist whom the complexity of natural form eludes and who must therefore simplify nature, converting all shapes into more legible bits of ornament.

It is true that the artist fractions the objects into smaller units, each of distinct shape. He seeks an articulation that is more like writing than like organic bodies; he renders a whole as if it were made up of strokes of the pen which form standard letters and punctuation, combined into words that build sentences which, taken together, constitute an ordered text.

What distinguishes it from a reductive style is that the vocabulary is so large and represents so many features of the real world. Each scene formed of such elements is a complex whole, with a structure that cannot be described like the elements through a simple, regular scheme. It owes its individual character, rather, to the conception of a unique meaning of the scene which is expressed through this whole.

The powers of expression latent in this method may be seen in the drawing of the four hands. Simple in design, almost childlike in the uniform repetition of the fingers, they exhibit a reflective concept of form. There is a scale of qualities in the contrast of the open and closed hand, the pointing and holding hand, as if this standardized unit contained many modalities of expression, like the tones of the keyboard. Besides, the careful study of the structure of the open hand—the marking of the joints, the muscles of the palm, the fingernails—convinces us that this artist has looked at his own hand with a desire to render it more truthfully. Through the choice of elements and flexibility of groupings, the artist affirms a master's freedom in spite of the naïveté and stereotyped nature of his elements.

Within the limits imposed by the general conception and by the subjects, which are mainly themes of ceremony, speech and confrontation rather than of dramatic action, there are some highly expressive gestures and postures. These are not merely conventional signs but owe their force to the evocative power of lines and contrasts. Slight changes in the standard form of a figure become attributes of feeling, the momentary states of figures reacting emotionally to each other. In the debate between Ildefonsus and Jovinianus, the heretic clutches his forked black beard, a sign of great tension,[29] while his follower, in a stiff contrapposto, turns his feet away though still looking at Ildefonsus. On the other side, the saint and his monk-follower preserve a contrasting unity of posture: vertical, parallel bodies, reinforced by the strict axis of the crozier (Fig. 4). Else-

29. For the clutching of the forked black beard as a sign of extreme tension, there is a moving example in the picture of Christ exorcising the demon of a possessed man in the Codex Aureus from Echternach in the Escorial: Albert Boeckler, *Das goldene Evangelienbuch Heinrichs III*, Berlin, 1933, pl. 79.

where, in the argument with the Jews, these relations are reversed (Fig. 6). It is the Jews who are rigidly recalcitrant and firm, with that *durities Judaeorum* so often denounced in the polemical literature of the Middle Ages; and it is the Christian Ildefonsus who betrays in his posture the stress of argument. Here he crosses his arms in speech, reversing their normal position, and holds the crozier at an unstable aggressive angle, while the Jew's staff is planted vertically in the exact center of the arched space between them.

The analytic character of this style, its persistent anatomizing of forms, is associated, then, with a mounting taste for reality.

What seems to us rigid in the single bodies—human and architectural—and repetitious in the design of details, is a chosen expressive form. The artist *can* draw and compose differently; we know that from other miniatures in the same series.

It is, I have said, mainly in the full-page paintings of figures in religious habit and in the context of architecture that the features of the style that I have described appear in their most decided character. In the smaller scenes the architecture is simpler—with columns and arcades but few exteriors of towers and roofs and no superposed structures (Figs. 7-14, 16, 18, 19).[30] The figures span the whole space between upper and lower borders. They are as tall as the largest elements of their surroundings and stand on a definite ground line (or band) instead of floating in space as in the full-page pictures; they often cross the borders and enter into the margin beyond it. Beside full-length figures there are many busts and half-length and three-quarter length figures. Some of these are framed by the borders and architecture as by an arcaded balcony or window (Figs. 11, 18, 19). With these changes in proportions and spacing, the whole acquires a less formal aspect, another atmosphere, without the solemnity of the full-page scenes. The image seems less knitted and firm and is more casually composed.

The individual figures, too, are conceived differently, though the elements are the same as in the large scenes. The expanded mantle, flaring at the sides, is a more frequent form (Figs. 7, 9, 12). The costume—not the architecture—fills out the space; there are fewer vertical accents and the horizontal relationships dominate the composition (Figs. 9, 16). In the absence of architecture, or with its reduction in size, the figures seem heavier, their thick dark contours and folds are more pronounced. Another aspect of the painter's art and temperament comes forth, his strength and certitude.

In some figures, the artist is a builder—not in stone, but like a master carpenter who joins big timbers to form a roof-tree, a dense criss-cross of diagonal, horizontal and vertical parts (Fig. 12).

In the full-page paintings (Figs. 1-3 and Colorplate 1) the governing symmetry of the clothed body, the stiffness of posture, the rhythmic lines of the folds that bind and close up the figure, create an image of the monk as an ideal type, a controlled existence subject to a rule by which the monk is completely defined.[31] The architecture is his exalted canopy, his tabernacle. The folds on his robe are insignia of spirituality and discipline; the lights between them, a delicate ornament of the severe heavy costume and an intimation of inwardness. With his small feet in black shoes, parallel and suspended, with his limited bodily articulation, noted before (Fig. 1) in the strange scheme of the knees—like a pair of eyes, passive and obedient—the monk is a creature of his order, an order that is tangible in the monastic building—the world of great embracing constructions and a strict rule of life.

In the smaller pictures (Figs. 7-14), another human type dominates—the Old Testament

30. The exceptions in Figs. 15, 17, 20 are much less complex than the full-page miniatures.

31. His bearing and form fulfill the prescriptions of a poem composed at Cluny in the 1040s: "Be silent, humble, most gentle and kind, / Guileless and docile, wise and modest in mind." ("Sit tacitus, humilis, mitissimus atque benignus. / . . . Indolis et docilis, sapiens et mente pusillus, / . . . Vivere cum Domino semper, et esse suo." B. Albers, *Consuetudines Monasticae*, Stuttgart-Vienna, 1, 1900, p. 136.

prophets. They stand on legs with opposed and balanced axes, with feet of flesh and bone, each turned differently—one foreshortened, the other in profile—true to the pagan norm of the self-adjusting body in Hellenic art. Their flaring mantles and the contrast of freer and more enveloped limbs accord with their greater range of religious action, their outspokenness and spontaneity. Though endowed with an apparent liberty, these prophet figures are more conventional in type, reviving old schemes of draping and modeling. The monk figure is a more recent creation, fitted to and determining an architectural unity which is not simply a construction of stone, but an inhabited structure, the monastery as a collective milieu.

We see better through this contrast that the monk figure is only one of several roles or types available to this artist; but the monk seems to be the one for whom the painter is able to conceive the most original expressive wholes and to exploit most deeply the resources of his art in composing figures and architecture.

The difference between the two sets of miniatures, all by the same artist, is remarkable. We observe here how a painter adapts to special conditions of content and how meaningful to a Romanesque artist is the scale of his work. The second group includes two miniatures with Ildefonsus (Figs. 13, 20), so that the difference does not depend on the presence or absence of this figure; it has more to do with the conception of the whole painting as an image-world, in the one case representing the collective-monastic sphere, in the other, individuals in a less organized world—the prophets of the Old Testament and their Jewish hearers.

There are a few scenes in which the artist has found solutions different from the two poles of form that I have described; they show his freedom of invention or perhaps only inherited resources of his art which include devices not employed in the other scenes. One is the painting of the prophet Micah who stands before the city—a giant figure, with head and halo framed by a great arch, while the tiny heads of the people whom he addresses emerge from behind the walls (Fig. 17). The rendering of the city, an architecture unique in the codex, is boldly adapted to the contrasted scales of prophet and community and to the space of the painted field. A second arch, of greater span than the first and springing from the same column, is cut by the upper frame; of the two columns supporting the prophet's arch, one descends to his feet, the other passes behind the walls of the town—a strong, naïve fitting of spatial elements that we have observed already in the other pictures. But we are struck also by the highly organized and contemporary aspect of the city, with the strict symmetry of the walls and the distinctive form of each story, in contrast to the composition of the painting as a whole.

Another example is the miniature of Jacob Blessing his Sons, an extremely rare subject in medieval art (Fig. 15). Though the gold inscription above the scene refers to the blessing of all the sons, Jacob points to Judah; for it is the blessing of Judah that contains the prophecy of Christ's coming which is quoted in the text below.[32] The painting fills only part of the page; it is placed above six lines of writing which are framed by an additional inner border. The features

32. In the Ashburnham Pentateuch (Paris, B.N.N.A. lat. 2334, Ph. Lauer, *Les enluminures romanes de la Bibliothèque Nationale*, Paris, 1927, pl. I) the essential theme is Jacob blessing the sons of Joseph. Closer to the theological idea of the Parma miniature, but rendered differently to illustrate the symbolism, is the panel in the Klosterneuburg altar by Nicholas of Verdun. Jacob points with his staff to two lions (as if to awaken them) to signify the lion of Judah from which redemption will come. It is between the scenes of Samson and the Lion and Christ's Resurrection. Jacob's scroll reads: "Nos redimens agnus ex Juda fit leo magnus" (To redeem us the lamb becomes a great lion out of Judah's race). Only two sons stand beside Jacob. Closer to the Cluny miniature in composition is the painting of the 13th century in the John Rylands Library, Manchester, MS fr. 5, fol. 44 (R. Fawtier, *La Bible historiée tout figurée de la John Rylands Library*, Paris, 1924, pl. XL), where Jacob, in bed, raises his hand in speech, and the twelve sons stand behind him in two rows. But the special reference to Judah is lacking here, as it is also in the related representation in the Smyrna Octateuch, where the brothers form two groups behind the reclining Jacob (see D. C. Hesseling, *Miniatures de l'Octateuque grec de Smyrne*, Leyden, 1909, no. 146).

Jacob's blessing and prophecy on Judah and Christ are cited by Fulbert of Chartres early in the 11th century in his treatise against the Jews (Migne, *Pat. lat.*, CXLI, cols. 308, 309, 314—"non auferetur sceptrum de Iuda"), and also by Odilo in a sermon (XII) on the Assumption of the Virgin (*ibid.*, CXLII, col. 1024).

of the twelve heads of the sons, and the recurrent lines of the costume, are related in thickness and articulation to the strokes that make up the letters below. But this group of figures, of which the relentless uniformity of the heads is not mitigated by the small variations of hair and beard among twelve brothers, possesses a depth and modeling unique in the manuscript. In the densely packed space there is no large golden void that defines a background plane as in the other scenes. Between the foreground, established by the patriarch and his bed, with the many planes of the bed clothes in pleated layers and of the space of the body and the extended arms—between this foreground space and the architecture in the background, the sons are aligned in a hemicycle of six figures behind whom stand the others, partly within, partly in front of the gabled building. The towers at the sides, rendered as cylinders by light and shadow, also give a measure of depth. One can distinguish at least six, perhaps seven, planes in depth. The upper row of heads is smaller and partly covered by the brothers in front, whose heads cut off the lower parts of five faces; one head belonging to neither row is set between the two groups at the right. The front series around Jacob would alone be enough to suggest a considerable depth. Judah's head, at the right, is the largest of all; the diminution of heads, as well as of the collars, toward the center of the group is an appreciable change—a startling example of perspective in the art of ca. 1100. In the conception of the crowd there is still a residue of late classical composition that survives also in Byzantine and Ottonian art. We would expect in this manuscript, which is governed to so high a degree by a clarifying analytic method of representation—typical of many Romanesque works—that all the heads would be equally large and equally complete.[33] The common practice of the time may be illustrated by the reliefs of the cloister of Santo Domingo de Silos, where the twelve apostles are drawn in superposed groups, with each head fully visible.[34] As in Silos, a regard for symmetry has led the artist to divide the groups with respect to a vertical axis; on and near this axis the painter of Cluny has extended arms and hands in crossing and contrasting gestures that oppose their spontaneity to the set arrangement of the repeated heads and bodies, yet possess a carefully designed rhythm of which the elements are bound also to the neighboring lines of the costume. The large figure of Jacob, the only one that is shown in full length, pulls the whole composition to the left, confounding the symmetry and the architectural axes of the rest; but the central building, with its luminous gable turned to the left, restores the balance and "justifies" Jacob's extended gestures, the straight and bent arms which resemble the forms of gable and roof. This rigid left arm across the field, pointing to Judah, recalls the corresponding diagonal arms breaking the regularity of the scene in the Doubting Thomas and the Deposition of Christ at Silos.

Returning to the broad contrast of the more and the less architectural miniatures in the Parma Codex, we note that both correspond to features of the new sculpture of that time. The first miniatures, which are so highly formalized, make us think of the constructive aspect of monumental art; the second suggest—though in a limited degree—the expansive energy of Romanesque representation, the liberty of invention in drapery forms and postures in the same architectural reliefs.

What the painter of the Parma manuscript does in the smaller pictures, simplifying the architecture and reducing it to the size of the figures, and endowing these with a greater flexibility of form, may be compared to a sculptor's transformations in passing from a tympanum to a frieze or lintel. The first has qualities that belong to a centralized theme of state in which the archivolt participates as closure, echo or reinforcement, though a figure may also, as in the eruptive form of the central tympanum of Vézelay, break through the frame; the second becomes a field of multiple action, unconstrained by a prior frame or setting.

33. The costumes look more "Romanesque" than in the other scenes; note especially the beaded collar and vertical strip on the breast of the second son from the right.

34. See ART BULLETIN, XXI, 1939, p. 337, fig. 17 (Doubting Thomas), p. 346, fig. 29 (Pentecost), and Porter, *Spanish Romanesque Sculpture*, I, pls. 36, 39.

In the Parma manuscript the second type might even be described as, in a sense, unframed, in spite of the rectangular enclosure. The figures have an independent existence, and the frame is put around them once they have taken their places in a reserved field. This frame does not enclose the figure, but isolates it as a whole or part—observe how in Fig. 18 Habakkuk is set between two frames, standing in front of the inner one, which contains the column and the plant, and behind the outer frame which encloses the whole text (cf. also Fig. 11). While in the first set of pictures the frames and the buildings seem to be there from the start, in the second group there occur frames which, in responding to a single encroaching letter of the adjoining text, make a detour around it and break the regularity of the rectangle enclosing the figure.[35] In the scene of Jacob Blessing his Sons (Fig. 15), the writing below it cuts into the frame of the page.[36]

The characteristic flexibility of Romanesque design, which points to future art, appears in Parma as an essential trait in the work of this painter. In contrast to the notion of canonical forms of figure and frame it suggests an empirical attitude which is prepared to modify the general and ideal in adapting to the contingent.[37] It seems to be rooted in the plural values of the figure—a creature of action with an independent range and freedom, as well as part of a system of church, monastery, or religious community, which imposes bonds between the figures and exalts or constrains them, in tying them to the collective form that is the great multiplex building.

The difference between the two series of paintings, all by the same artist, is not explained by the supposition, plausible as it may be, that the first depends on a German imperial manuscript with an elaborate architectural setting and ornamented frames, while the second corresponds to a plainer, more straightforward native art. For though such dependence might account for the greater richness of the first set of miniatures and for certain elements, it does not explain the specific conception of the unity of figures and architecture which I have described, a conception that is not found in the Ottonian treasure manuscripts and accords rather with contemporary Romanesque art.

We may interpret this style as an expression of the sensibility shaped by the Cluniac way of life in the monastic institution—admitting the vagueness of such analogies. The greatest intensities of the figures are gestural and ritualistic; their postures are determined by their religious role; they are figures who listen, pray, argue and affirm, who stand for Christian, Jew or heretic. There is no great spontaneity or drama here, no deep inner life, only a prescribed dialogue, ceremony, or prayer. Cluny is a world absorbed by the performance of rites; it is also a model of communal order, with its powerful abbot, dependent priors, and disciplined monks supported by great possessions. As such, Cluny is respected by kings, emperors and popes, and consulted by them; it has achieved a stable centralized form and it favors such forms in society at large. By 1100 its reforming initiative is over; it has become a kind of Byzantium of the West, in the religious rather than secular order of life—conservative, strict in liturgical etiquette, cultivated though unenterprising intellectually, but most energetic in church-political affairs and in promoting the arts of building and decoration that magnify the image of the monastery in the outer world. Its third church (of 1088-ca. 1115) is a rival of St. Peter's in Rome and an inspiration in the development of stone sculpture, which gives a new, more commanding face to religion in the growing secular sphere. But in philosophy, science, theology, law, poetry, history, as in economic practice, Cluny is backward or insignificant beside the most active centers of that period, though it possesses one of the greatest libraries of Europe.

35. Cf. fols. 27v, 38v (Fig. 29).

36. The frame gives way before "princeps," a sign that here the text preceded the painting of the frames. Elsewhere (fols. 44, 70v, etc.) the writing sometimes crosses the upper border.

37. This is not intended as a complete account of the types of frame-field-figure relations in Romanesque art. I have discussed this aspect of Romanesque sculpture elsewhere: "Über den Schematismus in der romanischen Kunst," *Kritische Berichte zur kunstgeschichtlichen Literatur*, Zürich-Leipzig, 1932-1933, pp. 1-21.

CHAPTER VII

THE ILDEFONSUS PAINTER AND GERMAN ART

THERE can be little doubt that this Cluniac style, particularly in the full-page paintings, depends for many of its features on German art of the eleventh century. I shall list a series of elements and their counterparts in German art which confirm the impression we receive from these Cluniac miniatures as a whole. What is uncertain is the center from which the models came and the time of their reception in Cluny. Was there in Cluny an illustrated German manuscript, a gift of one of the emperors, that served as a model? Shall we suppose also a broader acquaintance with German art and a continuous practice of its forms at Cluny in the eleventh century? For the style of Hand A has much in common not only with Ottonian art of the end of the tenth and the first quarter of the eleventh century, but also with German manuscripts of the late eleventh; there are resemblances to the art of Western Germany and equally striking affinities with Bavarian painting as well. To demonstrate the close connections with German Imperial art, one can point to the works made in Regensburg for Henry II, formerly Duke of Bavaria, and for Henry IV, or to the manuscripts produced in Echternach in the second and third quarter of the eleventh century for Henry III and Conrad. Since the abbots Odilo and Hugo were friends of these monarchs and Burgundy belonged to the empire, such connections of style, particularly in a luxury manuscript in gold and purple, are not surprising. Odilo's biographer, Jotsaldus, speaks of the precious gifts of the German emperors to Cluny; and in another context he mentions a sacramentary written in letters of gold that was lost and recovered on a journey of Odilo.[38]

Although this exceptional type of manuscript, with text as well as full-page paintings framed by borders of acanthus and meander ornament, goes back to Carolingian imperial works like the Codex Aureus of Charles the Bald in Munich (Staatsbibl. lat. 14000), which was preserved and copied in Regensburg, it is unlikely that the style of the old Carolingian models, whether of East or West Frankish origin, affected Cluny by way of native French art. I do not know of French manuscripts of the eleventh century with this conception of the sumptuous illustrated book in purple and gold. Besides, many of the details that I shall mention in comparing the Parma Codex with German art belong not to the Carolingian style, but to Ottonian art of the later tenth and eleventh centuries. Even if one supposed that monk-painters from a German center brought their style to Cluny, one must also assume that an elaborate German manuscript, a gift from an emperor to Cluny, served as a model for the sumptuous features of the codex. The text of Ildefonsus in itself could hardly have inspired this splendor of execution; it has been written and decorated with a luxury reserved then for the most important service books of the church—the gospels, sacramentaries and psalters. In the Parma manuscript the succession of a recto page with a title or incipit in gold capitals on purple ground, the verso with a full-page miniature on a gold ground, followed by a recto with a large gold initial letter on purple, already points to an imperial Germanic model. The division of the first pages of Ildefonsus' text into sections that make possible a series

38. Migne, *Pat. lat.*, CXLII, cols. 902, 904, 931. See also Radulfus Glaber, *ibid.*, CXLII, cols. 625, 626, on the imperial globe, crown and scepter given to Cluny by Henry II. In the *Consuetudines Farfenses*, which were composed at Cluny about 1040-1049, are recorded the verses inscribed on sacred vessels given by the same emperor: "Uodilo nomen habens haec vasa patraverat abbas / Heinrici regis et munere contulit aris" (Albers, *Consuetudines Monasticae*, I, p. 183). In the same work are mentioned liturgical manuscripts bound in gold, silver, and gems, which are set up for display on the altar on major feast-days (*ibid.*, p. 82). For the relations of Cluny and the later emperors, note the entry: "depositio domni Chonradi regis et Heinrici ducis amicorum nostrorum" in the martyrology of Cluny, recorded in the same *Consuetudines* (p. 205). For Hugo's friendship with Henry III and with his godson, Henry IV, see the biographies of Hugo by Hildebert and others, Migne, *Pat. lat.*, CLIX, cols. 857, 864, 893, 917ff.

of four full-page miniatures, each facing a large initial, suggests that a manuscript of the gospels or an evangeliary has inspired the artist.[39] The system of division is not maintained in the rest of the manuscript, however; many smaller miniatures are inserted in the following text, as in evangeliaries of the middle and later eleventh century from Regensburg, Salzburg, and Echternach. The illustration of the colophon, we shall see later, reflects a model with scribe and presentation scenes at the end, as in Echternach.

The Regensburg manuscripts made for Henry II, as well as the books produced at Echternach for his successors, do not correspond closely to the scheme of decoration in the Parma Codex. In the earlier Regensburg books the borders, which are copied from the Codex Aureus, are far more elaborate, with squares, lozenges and medallions breaking the rectangle of the frame.[40] The imperial manuscripts of Echternach show still another system of decorative pages and ornament. On the other hand, there is a resemblance to manuscripts from less important Bavarian centers, like Freising and Tegernsee, that depend on Regensburg;[41] but these manuscripts lack the richly framed text and the gold and purple incipit pages of the Parma Codex. We might postulate the existence in Cluny of a gospel book of the last quarter of the eleventh century, produced at Regensburg for the emperor Henry IV, imitating the framed text of the Codex Aureus, at a time when the style of Regensburg was closest to that of the Cluny manuscript.[42] But for this we have no strong evidence.[43]

Here are some obvious features found in both the Ildefonsus Codex and German art, which apparently came to Cluny directly from the German schools rather than from a common or mediating source.

a. The figures set in a field of architecture, showing interior and exterior together and touching the frame. For the German examples, see the Registrum Gregorii in Trier,[44] the Echternach Pericope Book of Henry III now in Bremen,[45] St. Gall Stiftsbibliothek MS 340,[46] the Bavarian manuscript Bamberg, Staatl. Bibliothek Lit. 2,[47] and the Liège Sacramentary, Paris, Bibl. Nat. lat. MS 819.[48]

b. Superposed buildings enclosing the figures. The effect is of an interior with several stories, or of a complex of neighboring structures like a monastery or town. Compare the Echternach Gospels in Paris (Bibl. Nat. lat. MS 10438)[49] and manuscripts from Regensburg (the Uta Codex and the Vatican Gospels of Henry II—Ottobonianus lat. 74).[50]

c. Openwork effect of arcades. This is strikingly as in the manuscripts from Regensburg.[51] In a Bavarian manuscript, Munich Clm. 2939,[52] the whole scene rests on a lower arcade, as in the Parma Codex, fols. 1v, 4v, 9v (Figs. 1, 3, and Colorplate 1).

d. Convergence of buildings toward a center (Fig. 4). A remarkably similar form appears in St. Gall, Stiftsbibliothek 390 (Fig. 67).[53]

39. This division is not found in the original copy by Gómez (Paris, B.N. lat. 2855) nor in the other Cluniac copies.

40. Swarzenski, *Regensburger Malerei*, pls. VII-XXI *passim*.

41. E. Bange, *Eine Bayerische Malerschule des XI. und XII. Jahrhunderts*, Munich, 1923.

42. Cf. the Gospel Book of Henry IV in Cracow (Swarzenski, *Regensburger Malerei*, pls. XXXIII-V, nos. 92-101).

43. The Echternach codices, too, lack the framed text. But the model might have come from one of several West German centers that owned works of the Carolingian Court school—see note 111 below and pp. 31, 32.

44. Goldschmidt, *German Illumination*, II, pl. 7.

45. Goldschmidt, *German Illumination*, II, pl. 52.

46. A. Merton, *Die Buchmalerei in St. Gallen*, Leipzig, 1923, pl. 80.

47. Bange, *Eine Bayerische Malerschule*, fig. 62. Cf. also the Bavarian or Swabian miniature formerly in Maihingen, Cod. I, 2.IV° 11, *ibid.*, fig. 48 (our Fig. 61).

48. M. Schott, *Zwei Lütticher Sakramentare in Bamberg und Paris und ihre Verwandten* (Zur Geschichte der Lütticher Buchmalerei im XI. Jahrhundert), Strassburg, 1931, figs. 12, 13; cf. also the sacramentary, Bamberg, Staatsbibl. Lit. 3, *ibid.*, figs. 4, 5.

49. Goldschmidt, *German Illumination*, II, pl. 51. The manuscript was preserved in Metz.

50. Goldschmidt, *German Illumination*, pl. 76 (Uta), 78 (Ottob. 74).

51. Goldschmidt, *German Illumination*, *loc.cit.* and Swarzenski, *Regensburger Buchmalerei*, pls. XII, XIV, XV, XIX, XXI.

52. Bange, *Bayerische Malerschule*, figs. 160, 161, 163–but the general effect is different. Cf. also Munich lat. 18005, 6204, 23343, and Bamberg, Staatsb. Lit. 2, where the evangelist's seat rests on an arcade (*ibid.*, figs. 9, 37, 115, and 62).

53. The Antiphonary of Hartker (986-1017); Merton, *Die Buchmalerei in St. Gallen*, pl. 67[2]. There is an earlier

e. Knobbed spires, domes, and gables, aligned horizontally. These occur in both Echternach[54] and Bavaria.[55]

f. Rectangular arches, which may be described also as stilted lintels (Colorplate I and Figs. 4, 5)—a Carolingian form which goes back, I believe, to Italian works of the preceding period and ultimately to Egyptian art, where they are a common feature in the temples of the Ptolemaic and Roman periods (Dendera, Philae).[56] They are found later in Ottonian works, e.g., Munich Clm. 4452 from Reichenau.[57]

g. Capitals of compact basket shape, convex, with close-fitting half-leaves at the sides—a simplified acanthus, trilobed and paired symmetrically, sometimes with a small shrub or wedge between them (Figs. 3, 8). Similar forms appear in manuscripts of Salzburg and Regensburg[58] toward the end of the eleventh century; they seem to be Romanesque reductions of an older, more plastic type found in late Carolingian and West German Ottonian miniatures.[59] The type goes back to a late classic form, as in the consular diptych of Probianus (Berlin) which comes from Werden and served as a cover of an Ottonian book.[60]

h. Figures suspended in the space of the buildings, having no contact with a continuous ground or base line. Cf. the benedictional of Swabian or Bavarian origin formerly in Maihingen (Fig. 61).[61]

i. Folds rendered as regular curved lines in series. These are typical in Regensburg and other Bavarian centers since the early eleventh century and continue into the twelfth; they give to Bavarian art a precociously Romanesque aspect. Compare the Uta Codex and Ottob. 74,[62] the Gospel Book of Henry II in Bamberg,[63] and later manuscripts of Salzburg.[64] But this tendency of Ottonian art may be found also in Western German centers, e.g., the Poussay evangeliary from Reichenau (Bibl. Nat. lat. 10514)[65] and manuscripts of St. Gall,[66] Einsiedeln,[67] and Echternach.[68] It is a general Western form arising independently, it seems, in different centers,[69] and has diagnostic value only in connection with less common features.

Carolingian example in a South German manuscript, Innsbruck University, codex 484, gospels from Innichen (Goldschmidt, *German Illumination*, I, pl. 52).

54. Cf. the Codex Aureus in Madrid (Escorial); A. Boeckler, *Das goldene Evangelienbuch*, pl. 61. Cf. also St. Gall MSS 338 and 340; Merton, *Die Buchmalerei in St. Gallen*, pl. 80.

55. Cf. the Bertolt manuscript from Salzburg; Swarzenski, *Regensburger Malerei*, pls. XXVIII-XXXII.

56. See my remarks in ART BULLETIN, XXXIV, 1952, p. 149. See also page 37 below on the later Italian examples in connection with fol. 102v.

57. See Goldschmidt, *German Illumination*, II, pl. 37. Cf. also St. Gall, Stiftsbibl. MS 340 (Merton, *Die Buchmalerei in St. Gallen*, pl. 78), Paris, B.N. lat. 10514, the evangeliary from Poussay, written in Reichenau (H. V. Sauerland and A. Haseloff, *Der Psalter Erzbischof Egberts von Trier*, Trier, 1901, pl. 55, no. 2), and the wall painting of the Resurrection of Lazarus in St. George in Oberzell, Reichenau (G. Dehio, *Geschichte der deutschen Kunst*, 3rd ed., I, 1923, fig. 356).

58. Cf. Swarzenski, *Regensburger Malerei*, pls. 34, 35, fig. 95 (Cracow, Evangeliary of Henry IV), pls. 28-32, figs. 76, 79, 82, 90 (the Bertolt manuscript from Salzburg, now Pierpont Morgan Library, New York, MS 780).

59. Cf. Innsbruck, University, MS 484, from Innichen, s. IX, 2 (Goldschmidt, *German Illumination*, I, pl. 52); Munich, Staatsbibliothek lat. 14345, s. IX, from Regensburg? (*ibid.*, I, pl. 53); Aachen Cathedral, Gospels of Otto III (*ibid.*, II, pl. 2); Egbert Codex, Trier MS 24 (*ibid.*, II, pl. 4, plain basket form without ornament); the Lorsch gospels (*ibid.*, II, pl. 18A); Cologne Cathedral MS 218 (*ibid.*, II, pl. 41); Munich, Staatsbibliothek lat. 4456 (*ibid.*, II, pl. 74); Hildesheim, Guntbald gospels (*ibid.*, II, pl. 103). For a similar form in Burgundy, cf. the sculptured capital on the altar at Avenas (Porter, *Romanesque Sculpture*, fig. 15).

I note here as a parallel to the Romanesque reduction in Regensburg, Salzburg, and Cluny the capitals represented in the mosaics of Joseph in the atrium of San Marco at Venice (S. Bettini, *Mosaici antichi di Venezia*, Bergamo, 1944, pls. 82-86).

60. See H. Schnitzler, *Rheinische Schatzkammer*, Düsseldorf, 1957, pls. 160, 161.

61. Bibl. Öttingen-Wallerstein, Cod. I, 2.IV°, 11 (Bange, *Bayerische Malerschule*, fig. 48); cf. also the Gero Codex (Reichenau), Goldschmidt, *German Illumination*, II, pl. 17; the Registrum Gregorii, *ibid.*, pls. 7, 8.

62. Goldschmidt, *German Illumination*, pls. 76, 77, 78; cf. also Paris, B.N. lat. 1231 (pontifical of Regensburg, 1060-1089), Swarzenski, *Regensburger Malerei*, pl. XXXII; Cracow, Gospels of Henry IV, *ibid.*, pls. XXXIII-V, figs. 92-101.

63. Swarzenski, *Salzburger Malerei*, figs. 26, 27.

64. *Ibid.*, figs. 29-31 (Munich 15904–evangiles from Stift Nonnberg), figs. 34, 36, 38, 40 (Michelbeuern evangiles), 33, 35, 37, 39 (gospels from St. Peters, Salzburg).

65. Goldschmidt, *German Illumination*, II, pl. 22 (also the Gero Codex, *ibid.*, II, pl. 17), and Sauerland and Haseloff, *Psalter Erzbischof Egberts*, pls. 53-55.

66. Cf. Merton, *Die Buchmalerei in St. Gallen*, pls. LIV,2, LXIII,1.

67. Cf. E. T. DeWald, "The Art of the Scriptorium of Einsiedeln," ART BULLETIN, VII, 1925, pp. 79ff. and figs. 33 (Einsiedeln MS 167), 35, 36 (MS 176).

68. Goldschmidt, *German Illumination*, II, pls. 43-61 *passim*, and especially pl. 58.

69. For an early example, ca. 800, cf. Amiens MS 18, a psalter from Corbie (V. Leroquais, *Les psautiers manuscrits des bibliothèques publiques de France*, Paris, 1937, pls. III-VI).

j. The gabled imperial crowns with knobs at the three angles (fols. 26v, 41, Fig. 8). This un-French type is represented in images of the German rulers; examples are known in Bavarian and West German works made for Henry II, III, IV, and Conrad. Those in Echternach manuscripts are closest to the type in Parma.[70]

k. The Jewish hats (Figs. 6, 7) are known first in German representations from Reichenau and Augsburg;[71] but I cannot say how general this usage was and from what center it spread throughout Europe.

l. The forms of the seat and writing stand, with seat elevated on an arcaded pedestal (Colorplate 1), are familiar in Bavarian miniatures.[72]

m. Ildefonsus writing, with the open book on the lectern (Colorplate 1), is based on a type of evangelist portrait common in German art and descended from a Carolingian model like the Matthew in the Vienna Schatzkammer Coronation gospels. A similar baluster-shaped writing stand, with foliate capital and base, occurs in the Bavarian manuscript, Munich Clm. 12201a.[72a]

For the question of a specific source as distinguished from the general spread of Ottonian forms, it should be kept in mind that if the Parma Codex in many respects resembles South East German manuscripts, the latter themselves depend on West German art, as investigators of Ottonian art ascertained long ago in their pioneer studies.[73] While Cluny had relations with Bavaria through the extension of its monastic reform to the imperial abbey of St. Emmeram at Regensburg, the movement of reform pursued by Cluniac monks was strongest in the west of the Empire, in part through the independent action of their followers at Gorze, Stavelot, Echternach, and Trier, and later at Hirsau in Swabia.

To discern, then, the precise connections of Cluny with German art, it is necessary to look beyond the obvious similarities of widely used detail and to consider the more distinctive aspect of the whole. In the Cluniac style much that was taken from Germany is already transformed, yet it has been possible for a German scholar in describing a manuscript of Echternach to characterize it in broad terms that seem to apply to the Parma miniatures as well. Dr. Peter Metz, writing on the Golden Codex from Gotha, found in the art of Echternach a foretaste of scholastic rationalism,

70. Cf. Bamberg, Staatl. Bibl. 95 (A.II.46), pericope book from Seeon for Henry II (Goldschmidt, *German Illumination*, II, pl. 79); Cracow, cathedral chapter library MS 208, Gospels of Henry IV, from Regensburg? (J. Prochno, *Das Schreiber- und Dedikationsbild in der deutschen Buchmalerei*, I, Leipzig-Berlin, 1929, pls. 95, 96 and Swarzenski, *Regensburger Malerei*, pl. XXXIII); Madrid (Escorial), Codex Aureus, for Henry III (1043-1046), from Echternach, Goldschmidt, *op.cit.*, II, pl. 58; Upsala University library, Gospels of Goslar, Echternach, 1050-1056, crowning of Henry III, *ibid.*, pl. 63; Nuremberg, Codex Aureus from Echternach, Herod in Massacre of the Innocents (P. Metz, *Das Goldene Evangelienbuch*, Munich, 1956, colorplate VI, pl. 31); Paris, B.N. lat. 11961, fols. 7v, 8, gospels from Echternach, second half of 11th century; Berlin, Staatl. Bibl. theol. fol. 358, psalter from Werden, ca. 1100 (P. Clemen, *Die romanische Monumentalmalerei in den Rheinlanden*, Düsseldorf, 1916, fig. 498); seal of Conrad II.

In some examples from the Echternach school, the central vertical strip joining the apex to the diadem band is omitted, as in the Parma Codex; but this may simply be a later type, for it is found also in the later Bavarian example, the Gospels of Henry IV in Cracow. There is an approach to the early type in some manuscripts from Cluny: B.N.N.A. lat. 2390 (Fig. 63) and N.A. lat. 1450, fol. 39v (David); but what appears to be the gable is merely the outline of the hair. On the other hand, the early gabled type is found in Northern France: B.N. lat. 9654A, capitulary of Ansegis (827), 10th century (P. Schramm, *Die deutschen Kaiser und Könige*, I, fig. 9a), and in England: British Museum, Tiberius C VI, David (M. Rickert, *Painting in Britain, The Middle Ages*, Pelican History of Art, London, 1954, pl. 50), and the St. Albans psalter in Hildesheim (O. Pächt, C. R. Dodwell, and Fr. Wormald, *The St. Albans Psalter*, London, 1960, pls. 41, 73b). In the latter manuscript occurs also the later simpler type, as in Cluny (*ibid.*, pls. 21, 34).

The gabled form may be simply a convention for representing the circular diadem crown, a conflation of the horizontal band and the peaked "perspective" form.

71. Cf. Berlin, Kupferstichkabinett, MS 78.A.2, fol. 26v, Evangeliary of Henry IV, Reichenau school; Augsburg Cathedral, the prophets of the windows, ca. 1100 (G. Dehio, *Geschichte der deutschen Kunst*, fig. 388); Karlsruhe, Cod. Aug. 161, late 11th century, Bavarian; Düsseldorf, Landesbibl. MS D.4 (sacramentary of Essen); Stuttgart, Cod. Bibl. Fols. 57 and 60; Externsteine; Verona, San Zeno, bronze door (A. Boeckler, *Die Bronzetür von Verona*, Marburg, 1931, pp. 28, 29, with list of examples). A forerunner of this type is the hat in the miniature of Paul preaching in Einsiedeln MS 138, s.X,2 (DeWald, ART BULLETIN, VII, 1925, fig. 38, pl. LXV).

72. Cf. Munich, lat. 22044 (Bange, *Bayerische Malerschule*, fig. 153); lat. 6204 (*ibid.*, fig. 37, Freising); lat. 6832 (*ibid.*, fig. 58, Freising); lat. 12201a (*ibid.*, figs. 78, 79, 81, 84, Freising school), the clearest example. For an author-portrait with a similar arcaded pedestal, cf. Einsiedeln MS 167, s.X,2 (DeWald, ART BULLETIN, VII, 1925, fig. 33).

72a. Bange, *Bayerische Malerschule*, figs. 78, 79.

73. Swarzenski, *Regensburger Malerei*, pp. 54, 55, 117ff.; confirmed by Bange, *Bayerische Malerschule*, pp. 17, 18, 31, 37, 55.

a feeling for the highly organized form, which he connected with the spiritual influence of the Cluniac movement in Western Germany.[74] But one can find even earlier in the art of Regensburg, in such a work as the Uta Codex of Regensburg, a systematizing mode of composition in which the figures are set in a complex architecture and framed fields of different size are combined in a schematic hierarchic whole.

If we compare these works with the Cluny manuscript, they will appear, relative to the latter, more Ottonian than Romanesque in spite of the strong suggestion of the Romanesque in the simplicity and regularity of lines. In the Parma Codex the folds have become more pronounced as a continuous, strongly accented network of lines joining the contours; they are more like a construction, a curved grid. In the German paintings the folds are often seen as isolated marks or ridges on the colored mass of the figure. The art of Echternach is narrative in spirit and retains much of the older flecking and atmospheric tonality, though it has lost the Ottonian fervor of expression. Where Cluniac art is analytic, schematized, and constructive in rendering the conventual world of the monks, the Echternach style is loosely descriptive and the figures are less firmly assimilated to the building forms. In the Uta Codex, on the other hand, the content is more truly abstract than at Cluny, with many inscriptions, often metrical, explaining the pictured concepts, and with frequent personifications. The systematizing form in Regensburg has to do with ideas, with an analogical order; and the form of a page is that of a complex emblem, a framework of circles, squares, and lozenges, enclosing symbolic figures, each in a field of its own. An accompanying openwork architecture, rather skeletal and distinct from the system of assembled frames, provides a separate milieu for certain figures, but not a building that defines a space for the whole, as in Cluny. The whole in the German manuscript is indeed an expression of a school mode of thinking in which the emblematic pictures and the words have acquired a unity that is neither dramatic nor lyrical nor narrative, but theological.[75] What looks like a similar order in Cluny is not bound to abstract intellectual categories; it is the image of a unique moment and represents a concrete religious situation, though one which is permeated by the solemnities of ritual and monastic life. In illustrating a theological text the painter shows the human speakers in debate or prophetic address rather than as symbols of the spoken content.[76]

To all this must be added that the Parma miniatures are an original Burgundian work of about 1100, with newly invented themes and compositions. Its analytical method of drawing, its quasi-architectural grouping of repeated figures and its taste for strongly defined objects, are more characteristic of Romanesque than Ottonian art. If one is to seek parallels in German art for these qualities, they will be found sooner in works of the twelfth century or of the later years of the eleventh, which belong to the same stage of the Romanesque as the Parma Codex.[77] In a con-

74. Peter Metz, *Das goldene Evangelienbuch von Echternach im Germanischen National-Museum zu Nürnberg*, Munich, 1956, p. 97; see also pp. 77ff.

75. In both the Uta Codex and Ottob. 74 (the Gospels of Henry II) this schematic order of the whole does not exclude qualities of lively narrative and gesture in the separate scenes and figures; cf., for example, the little picture of an impending execution beneath the enthroned Henry II in Ottob. 74, which Prof. Herbert Bloch, in his admirable study of Monte Cassino art and history ("Monte Cassino, Byzantium and the West in the Earlier Middle Ages," *Dumbarton Oaks Papers*, Number 3, 1946, pp. 163-224), has connected convincingly with an actual event of 1022, thereby confirming a conjecture of G. Swarzenski; the scene recalls the image of the execution of the messenger at David's command in the Carolingian Bible of Charles the Bald in San Paolo fuori le mura in Rome. Such intensity of action is unknown in the Cluny manuscript, although it may be found in Burgundian Romanesque sculpture.

76. A rare example of the illustration of the prophetic content in the Parma Codex is the miniature of Fig. 18 with Habakkuk, the Lord, and the fig tree "that shall not blossom" (Habakkuk 3:17).

77. Cf. the later Bavarian manuscripts published by Bange, *Bayerische Malerschule*, figs. 35, 44, 45, 51, 56, 62ff., 78ff., 109-122, 127-130; these offer some suggestive similarities. The resemblance of the Parma miniatures to those in manuscripts of the late 11th century in Polish and Bohemian libraries seems to be due to their common German roots rather than to any direct connection; see F. Lehner, *Die böhmische Malerschule des XI. Jahrhunderts*, Prague, 1902, and *Czechoslovakia, Romanesque and Gothic Illuminated Manuscripts*, preface by H. Swarzenski, introduction by J. Květ, Unesco and New York Graphic Society, 1959, pls. I-IX, for the Vyšerad Codex in Prague; *Bulletin de la Société Française pour la reproduction des manuscrits à peintures*, 1935, pls. XXXVIII-XLI, the Gniezno evangeliary; *ibid.*, 1938, pls. I-IV, the Cracow, Czartoryski Museum, evangeliary. These Ger-

11. *Gómez presenting his copy to Bishop Gotiscalc*, Parma, Bibl. Palatina, MS lat. 1650, fol. 102v, ca. 1100

temporary miniature in a breviary from Liège (Munich Clm. 23261), Usener has noted the conversion of a native Ottonian model of the 1020's (Bamberg Staatsbibl. Lit. 3) into a Romanesque form, a process that may be likened to that in Cluny.[78] But if the new definiteness of the human and architectural forms recalls our manuscript, the specific relationships of figures and buildings that characterize Cluny are not found in this work from Liège. How far the similarity to later German art depends on the influence of one school upon another, how far it is the outcome of similar aims operating on common inherited forms, I am unable to say.

mano-Slavic works are provincial variants of Bavarian (and perhaps Saxon) art; cf. Clm. 18005 from Tegernsee, ca. 1030 (Bange, *Bayerische Malerschule*, figs. 7-10) and the Regensburg Gospels of Henry IV in Cracow (Swarzenski, *Regensburger Malerei*, pls. XXXIII-XXXV, nos. 92-101).

The tendency to more regular schematic forms with accented verticals may be found in Echternach toward 1100 (the Theofrid manuscript in Gotha), and also in Cologne in the second half of the 11th century, as in the Freiburg University, Bibl. MS 360a and the Abdinghof gospels (Goldschmidt, *German Illumination*, II, pls. 95, 96) about 1060.

78. For the fusion of Ottonian, late 11th century, and Byzantine forms to create a new Romanesque style in the Mosan region, see Karl Hermann Usener, "Das Breviar Clm. 23261 der Bayerischen Staatsbibliothek und die Anfänge der romanischen Buchmalerei in Lüttich," *Münchner Jahrbuch der bildenden Kunst*, 1950, I, pp. 78-92, and especially pp. 83ff.

CHAPTER VIII

THE INITIALS

THE dependence on German art is clearest in the large decorated initials, though here, too, the immediate source is uncertain. From the d on fol. 5 (Colorplate 1), in which the painter of the neighboring miniatures has drawn the figures of Christ and Ildefonsus, we judge that all the initials are by the same hand as the miniatures.

The initials are traced in red outlines; the basic letter form is in gold; the stems, leaves and trefoils in gold or silver; the blossoms and ties in silver; and all are set on a contrasting inner ground of light blue and green and an outer ground of purple. In places this inner ground, broken into reserved spots of cool light color, appears to be a part of the initial, an inlay rather than a ground, and adds a note to the scale of luminosities, as well as a degree of opaqueness, between the gold and purple.

Little collars with an ornament of dots hold the split shafts and bows of the letter together, and stems sometimes pass through the clefts. In several initials a stem pierces another stem (Fig. 22) or an unsplit shaft. The wavy and spiral stems cross each other often; the secondary stems, of shorter span—there are as many as six in the A of Fig. 28—issue successively from the inner side of a major one and in crossing it form complementary or counter spirals of different curvature and span, each ending in a trefoil (Figs. 30, 32-35, Colorplate 1).

A late classic taste for the spiral rinceau—a spreading, organic, yet recurrently centered form—has been adapted to a Northern taste for the interlace: for crossing, entanglement and penetration. The natural luxuriance of curving foliage is combined with the metallic and artificial aspect of smoothly hammered bands and collars, like a bouquet fashioned by a goldsmith—a spiral grill with attached vegetation. With all the overlapping of stems and blossoms there is little effect of relief; the elements are perfectly flat. To the intricacy of the interlaced spirals is opposed the simplicity of the letter as a whole, restless but compact, a clearly silhouetted spot against a darker purple ground.

Admitting the German origin of the type, the questions that arise for us in studying this ornament are: a) from what German center did it reach Cluny, and b) at what point in the native development of Cluniac ornament? c) Are there distinctive features that belong to the Cluniac adaptation? d) What development does this ornament undergo in Cluny?

To give definite answers to all these questions would require a fuller study of German ornament than I have been able to make. I shall state some tentative conclusions.

a) This type of initial is so widespread in Ottonian art that a resemblance to the forms of a particular center is not by itself decisive for determining the source of the Cluniac examples. In the latter can be found similarities in color and design to initials from St. Gall, Reichenau, Trier, Echternach, Regensburg, Salzburg, and other Bavarian centers, particularly Tegernsee and Freising (Fig. 31),[79] which have learned from Regensburg.[80] Because the accompanying frames and miniatures resemble the Parma Codex, Bavarian initials seem at first the likely source of the Cluniac. But the Southeast German ones, in color and motifs, are themselves derived from schools in the West nearer to Cluny.[81] Their ornament appears earlier in St. Gall and Reichenau,[82] whence it spreads

79. Cf. Munich lat. 18005, gospels from Tegernsee, ca. 1030; Bange, *Bayerische Malerschule*, figs. 13-15 (our Fig. 31); Clm. 18121, psalter from Tegernsee, *ibid.*, fig. 17; Clm. 6204, gospels from Freising, *ibid.*, fig. 38 (with bust of angel in circular field of scroll, as in the Parma Codex, fol. 5, our Colorplate 1); and later examples from the Bavarian schools (*ibid.*, figs. 123, 125, 131–Clm. 828, etc.).

80. *Ibid.*, p. 24 and fig. 16 (Uta Codex).

81. As was noted by Swarzenski, *Salzburger Malerei*, p. 26.

82. Cf. the St. Gall Maccabees manuscript in Leyden (A. Schardt, *Das Initial*, Berlin, 1938, pp. 99, 100) and works from Einsiedeln nearby: E. T. DeWald, ART BULLETIN, VII, 1925, pp. 79ff., figs. 7, 8 (Einsiedeln MS 113), 40 (MS 156), 48 (MS 141). For Reichenau cf. the Gero Codex, Darmstadt

before the end of the tenth century to the Rhineland[83] and soon after to Bavaria.[84] Although I have not found in the Rhineland a type of page with a single large silhouetted initial quite like the pages in Parma, there are in the Echternach codices smaller decorated initials in the body of the text and foliate letters of a title or incipit, very close to the Cluniac forms.[85] But where the initial fills a framed page the Rhenish artists give it a more complex and open ornament. Both the simpler, compact initials from Echternach and the larger lack the collars of the stems, with five studs, which are so common in Cluny and Bavaria. These may be found, however, in the initials of Metz which depend on Rhenish art.[86] Perhaps in Cluny a first stage of the Germanic initial, borrowed from a Rhenish center, has been modified in the copying of a Bavarian codex.

b) In Cluny this ornament appears for the first time nearly a century after it had been established as a common type in Ottonian art. I know of no examples that can be placed before 1050. Its introduction in Cluny seems to date from Hugo's rule (1049-1109)—a surprising fact, since his predecessor, Odilo (994-1049), was a close friend of the German emperors and especially of Henry II with whom he exchanged gifts of works of art.[87] Other communication between Cluny and the German monasteries would imply an acquaintance with Ottonian art. About 1015 a German bishop, Meinwerk, in visiting Cluny with Henry II, took back with him to Paderborn thirteen monks to found a new monastery, and with them he brought several liturgical books from the mother abbey—a transaction that we suppose was not one-sided.[88] If this type of initial cannot be found in surviving manuscripts from Cluny before the second half of the century, one of its important elements, the spiral scroll with crossing of stems and even with penetrations, does occur in a Bible written for Odilo (Paris, Bibl. Nat. lat. 15176, fol. 421) during the latter part of his rule. By 1050 the Ottonian type of initial ornament had reached Burgundy, to judge by the manuscripts of St. Benigne at Dijon under the abbot Halinardus (1031-1046).[89] And there are traces of this Germanic style in manuscripts of the Jura region and Metz, where Cluny had strong interests.[90]

(Schardt, *op.cit.*, p. 103), the Heidelberg sacramentary (*ibid.*, p. 107), the Codex Egberti (Trier MS 24) and the Bamberg Apocalypse (Bibl. 140). The dotted trefoil, characteristic of the Cluniac and German initials of this type, appears together with the spiral rinceau on the border of an Anglo-Saxon miniature of 935-939 in Bede's Life of St. Cuthbert, Cambridge, Corpus Christi College MS 183 (D. T. Rice, *English Art 871-1100*, Oxford, 1952, pl. 47). This trefoil is distinct from the Hiberno-Saxon motif of the three dotted berries, which occurs on the same border.

83. Cf. Paris, B.N. lat. 8851 (Goldschmidt, *German Illumination*, II, pl. 16); B.N. lat. 10501, *ibid.*, II, pl. 15; Chantilly, Musée Condé, codex 1447 (C. Nordenfalk, *Münchner Jahrbuch der bildenden Kunst*, dritte Folge, I, 1950, p. 64, fig. 6); Walters Gallery, Baltimore, MS W.9, *ibid.*, fig. 7—all from Trier. For Echternach, cf. the golden codices in the Escorial and Nuremberg—Goldschmidt, *op.cit.*, II, pl. 49 A, B, and for more complete illustration, A. Boeckler, *Das goldene Evangelienbuch Heinrichs III*, pls. 13, 41, etc., and P. Metz, *Das goldene Evangelienbuch zu Nürnberg*, pls. 37, 43, etc. For similar initials in other Echternach manuscripts, see Boeckler, *op.cit.*, pls. 184, 187, 190, 205. For Echternach initials closer in time to Parma 1650, cf. Gotha MS I.70 (Liber Floridus of abbot Theofrid, ca. 1100) and MS I.1, a late 11th century Bible. Other West German examples are in the Bernward Bible in the Domschatz of Hildesheim (MS 61) and Vatican, Reg. lat. 15.

84. Besides the examples in notes 79 and 80 above, cf. the gospels in St. Peter's, Salzburg (Swarzenski, *Salzburger Malerei*, fig. 41) and the Michelbeuern gospels (*ibid.*, figs. 43, 44).

85. Cf. the Escorial Codex—Boeckler, *op.cit.*, pls. 33, 40, 59, 71, 97, 108, 124, 136.

86. For Bavaria, cf. the Uta Codex (Schardt, *Das Initial*, p. 165), Munich lat. 18005 (Bange, *Bayerische Malerschule*, figs. 13, 15), 18121 (*ibid.*, fig. 17), 6204 (*ibid.*, fig. 38), 12201a (*ibid.*, fig. 86). For a Metz initial, cf. Berlin, Phillips MS 1687 (J. Kirchner, *Beschreibende Verzeichnis der Miniaturen-Handschriften der Staatsbibliothek zu Berlin*, Leipzig, I, 1926, fig. 40). See notes 108 and 109 below for other parallels to details of the Cluny initials in West German books. However, a survey of initials, undertaken by my pupil, Dr. Betty Ann Weinshenker, led her to suppose a Bavarian model of the Cluniac initials.

87. The spiral rinceau with crossing stems appears already, late in Odilo's rule, in an initial of his Bible, Paris, B.N. lat. 15176, fol. 421, but with a different type of foliage and color.

On gifts of the emperor Henry II and his successors to Odilo, see notes 15 and 38 above. There is in the Bamberg library a manuscript of a commentary on Paul's Epistles (B.I.8) written at Cluny and presented by Odilo to Henry II, a surprisingly poor work with provincial ornament.

88. See Vita Meinwerci, *Mon. Germ. Hist. SS.*, XI, p. 118, cap. 28.

89. Cf. Berlin, Staatsbibl., Hamilton MS 481, fol. 97 (D) and Paris, B.N. lat. 11624 and 9518.

90. Cf. Paris, B.N. lat. 17006, fol. 79 (from the Savoy-Vosges region); lat. 823 (missal of Remiremont); lat. 9392 (from Senones in the Vosges); lat. 10500 (from Besançon); The Hague, Bibl. Meermann, MS 10 B 12, fol. 9v (from St. Vincent, Metz); Metz, Bibl. mun. (pre-war), MS 2, vol. 3, fol. 54 (Bible, s.XI,2), MS 14, fols. 147(A), 170(C), 185v (psalter, s.XI), MS 16, fol. 19v (lectionary, s.XI), MS 35, fols. 20v, 130 (gospels), MS 304, fols. 1, 5, 15 (recueil, s.XI).

Perhaps earlier examples that existed in Cluny have been lost.[91] In a cartulary of Cluny (Paris, Bibl. Nat. Nouv. Acq. lat. 1497-1498), begun in the last years of Odilo's rule and continued into the early twelfth century, we observe the replacement of an older style of initial ornament, with a looser knotting and foliage characteristic of the time of Odilo, by the new Germanic forms (Fig. 66).[92] (The intermittent and somewhat haphazard transcription of old charters in this cartulary keeps us from fixing precisely the moment of the change.) The two styles also exist side by side in another manuscript of Cluny (Paris, Bibl. Nat. Nouv. Acq. lat. 1455; Fig. 65) which we know to be later than Odilo, since in the title of a work by the abbot, copied in this manuscript, he is called saint.[93]

A possible clue to the transmission of Ottonian book ornament to Cluny is the activity of the scribe Albert the German, who was brought to Cluny from Trier by his father, Andreas, under abbot Hugo. Both became monks of Cluny. From an inscription in a magnificent jewel-covered copy of the Bible produced by Albert for the abbot Pontius (1109-1122), and now lost, we learn this story of father and son.[94] Andreas died in Cluny. His son's name appears on charters written during the last years of Hugo's rule.[95] Albert most probably learned the book arts at Cluny; but if the father was a scribe and illuminator, he would have brought with him the style of Trier of the middle or second half of the eleventh century.

c) In the Cluny manuscripts the initial-ornament of this common Ottonian type seems, on the whole, clearer, rounder and simpler than in the full-page West German examples which tend to become sinuous and intricate, with multiplied detail and many pointed angular forms.[96] Beside them, the most complex Cluniac initials look centered and balanced, with a closer, more regular fitting of the spirals and trefoils to the large framework of the letter.

A single detail may be taken as a distinctive Cluniac sign. In the manuscripts of the Burgundian abbey, the trefoils are often marked with an inverted curved V that connects the dotted or ringed centers of the three lobes—centers already drawn in the German works.[97] It arose perhaps as a graphic translation of the strokes of color that spot or model the trefoil in certain German manuscripts.[98] It resembles also the arrowhead unit beside two round lobes in a blossom that often appears beside the trefoil in West German initials. This pointed blossom is particularly common in Reichenau[99] and spreads to Bavaria[100] and the Rhineland.[101]

91. There is probably a connection with West German art in a drawing of s.XI,1, in Paris, B.N.N.A. lat. 2390, fol. 32 (our Fig. 63, martyrdom of Peter and Paul), a lectionary with readings for Cluny's main feasts—see page 55 below.

92. In N.A. lat. 1497, fol. 85, initial d, the trefoil with three dots appears in an appendage of an initial of the older Odilo type. The latter type continues fairly late in the century, to judge by B.N.N.A. lat. 638 (Udalric, *Consuetudines*, which must be later than ca. 1082). There are also residues of the old art beside the new initial forms in B.N. lat. 13875, fol. 24 (Bernard, *Consuetudines*, last quarter of the 11th century or the very end).

93. On fol. 134. To judge by the script the book was written in the third quarter of the century, soon after Odilo's death in 1049.

94. "Hunc librum scripsit quidam frater Cluniacensis, antea vero Treverensis, Albertus nomine. . . . Pater autem praedicti fratris, Andreas nomine, cum ipso Cluniacum venit, et ambo, scilicet pater et filius, sancto Spiritu cooperante, et cordum illorum illustrante, a S. Patre Hugone habitum religionis susceperunt. Sed pater iamiam in Cluniacum obiit in Domino. . . ." The text is published in M. Marrier and A. Duchesne, *Bibliotheca Cluniacensis* (1614), Mâcon, 1915, col. 1645. See also page 48 below.

95. See *Recueil des chartes de l'abbaye de Cluny*, formé par Auguste Bernard, complété, revisé et publié par Alexandre Bruel, Paris, 1876-1903, V, p. 213, no. 3862 (1107), p. 223, no. 3869 (1108).

96. For Echternach, see note 83 above, and for Reichenau, Schardt, *Das Initial*, pp. 114, 127, 136, 137, 140, 147.

97. For examples, cf. the manuscripts cited in notes 82 and 83 above.

98. Cf. the Gero Codex, Schardt, *op.cit.*, p. 103, and Munich lat. 4456, the Sacramentary of Henry II from Regensburg, *ibid.*, p. 161.

99. See Schardt, *op.cit.*, pp. 113, 114, 127, 135, 143, 147. For the connection of Reichenau and Cluny, note in the Heidelberg sacramentary (Schardt, *op.cit.*, p. 114) the unusual four-lobed, spool-shaped unit which appears in the center of the A on fol. 16 of the Parma Codex (fig. 28). In a mid-11th century book (Paris, B.N. lat. 11624) from St. Bénigne at Dijon, an abbey reformed by Cluny, the blossom forms include a trefoil supported by a curved V (fig. 62)—a familiar Reichenau motif (Schardt, *op.cit.*, pp. 104, 105).

100. Cf. the Freising sacramentary, Munich lat. 6421 (Schardt, *op.cit.*, pp. 111, 112) and also Munich lat. 18005 (Bange, *Bayerische Malerschule*, figs. 13-15). The motif appears in a collection of leaves from Cluny-Paris, B.N.N.A. lat. 2442, fol. 1.

101. Cf. the Nuremberg Codex Aureus—P. Metz, *Das goldene Evangelienbuch*, pl. 4.

From Cluny this tiny motif on the trefoil was transmitted to the art of Cluniac abbeys at Limoges, Moissac and Fleury.[102] It may well be a Cluniac invention since it is absent from some of the earliest Cluniac initials that reproduce the German prototypes and include the three dots or circles of the trefoil, which are later connected by the inverted V. The form in its special Cluniac aspect does not seem to be characteristic of any German school, though it occurs sporadically in Germany[103] and later in Italy,[104] perhaps through copying of Cluniac manuscripts. In a few early German books there is a related graphic form, but this too is exceptional: an inverted T or Y joins the centers of the lobes of the trefoil.[105] There is also the rare motif of a curved V in a trefoil, which is different, however, in its relation to the larger unit—the trefoil being set between two converging stems. This motif appears in both Echternach and Bavaria, but is absent in Cluny.[106]

This type of initial, with the inverted V of the trefoils, is the common one in the manuscripts of Cluny in the later eleventh century and the beginning of the twelfth (Figs. 41, 57, 65-66).[107] In time, it becomes increasingly dense, richer in repeated detail, more intricate and irregular (Figs. 58-60). The ties are treated like plastic members in the round, the leaves curl and turn in depth, the background is strewn with dotted circles,[108] the outlines of the lobes are often wavering, and blossoms of five and more lobes are introduced.[109] From this elaboration, which agrees with the general tendency in Romanesque ornament of the early twelfth century toward greater relief and modeling, no strong consistent new style arises; indeed the later examples show a slackness of design and execution that points to the decline of the school.[110] When compared to these later works, the initials of the Parma Codex, in their flatness, firm drawing, and simple legible patterns, are seen to belong to an early stage of the type.

102. Cf. Paris, B.N. lat. 743, fols. 86v, 94, Limoges breviary, late 11th century; B.N. lat. 5351, fol. 93 (Limoges); B.N. lat. 2388, fol. 1 (Moissac); B.N. lat. 2788, fol. 72 (from Fleury, but perhaps written at Cluny); Leyden, B.P.L. MS 82, fol. 14v, Juvenal, s.XI,2 (Burgundian?); B.N. lat. 4614 and 5672.

103. Cf. Trier, Stadtbibliothek MS 859, Bible, German, s.XI,2.

104. Cf. Vatican lat. 10511, the Bovino Bible (Garrison, *Studies in the History of Mediaeval Italian Painting*, I, Florence, 1953, fig. 73); Parma, Pal. 386, Bible (*ibid.*, fig. 83); Paris, B.N. lat. 7102, s.XII,2, Italian, medical; Ithaca, N.Y., Cornell University Library, MS B 12, Origen on Paul, s.XII,1, Italian.

105. Cf. Einsiedeln 156 (DeWald, ART BULLETIN, VII, 1925, opp. p. 86, fig. 40, pl. LXV); Munich lat. 22311, from St. Gall (Merton, *Die Buchmalerei in St. Gallen*, pl. 38); Vienna cod. 553, W. German, s.XI,1 (*Verzeichnis*, VIII, 2, p. 19, fig. 11); Vienna cod. 1845 (*ibid.*, fig. 17, and Swarzenski, *Salzburger Malerei*, fig. 68), Nuremberg, Codex Aureus (Metz, *Das goldene Evangelienbuch*, pl. 56); Munich lat. 828 (Bange, *Bayerische Malerschule*, fig. 126); Trier Domschatz Cod. 140 (*ibid.*, figs. 139, 140); Prague, Codex Vyšehrad (Lehner, *Die böhmische Malerschule*, pl. XXXII). Cf. also Florence, Laurenz. MS XXI, 33, Italian, gospels, ca. 1100. In the Limoges breviary, Paris, B.N. lat. 743, fol. 86v, both the V and T (inverted) forms occur, suggesting that Cluny knew the two forms at the end of the 11th century.

106. In the Nuremberg Codex Aureus (P. Metz, *op.cit.*, pls. 27, 28), the Uta Codex (Schardt, *op.cit.*, p. 6) and Vienna MS 1845, from Bamberg (*Verzeichnis*, VIII, 2, fig. 17). In the first two examples the form is not in an initial.

107. It is found in B.N.N.A. lat. 1455, lat. 1087, Arsenal 371, B.N. lat. 13875, N.A. lat. 1497, 1498, 2246, 2261, 2247, 1491, 1456 (fols. 1, 2), 1496, 1450, 1436; the order is roughly that of their time. For reproductions, see Mercier, *Les primitifs français*, pl. 88 (1450), pl. 91 (1455), 108 (2247), 109 (2247, 2261), 112 (1436), 113 (1496). B.N. lat. 3779 (Mercier, pls. 85, 86) is probably from St. Vincent at Châlons, and B.N.N.A. lat. 1439 (*ibid.*, pl. 88) is by an Italian artist, as Delisle, *Inventaire des Manuscrits de la Bibliothèque Nationale, Fonds de Cluni*, Paris, 1884, p. 45, has recognized.

108. The dotted circles (N.A. lat. 2247, 2261) occur already in the 10th century in the Codex Egberti, Trier 24, fol. 16v, which was made by Reichenau monks for the archbishop of Trier, perhaps in Trier itself. Cf. also Trier MS 859, an 11th-century Bible, and an evangelistary of the early 11th century in the treasure of Mainz Cathedral. The same motif appears, however, as a decoration of costume in a Cluny lectionary, B.N.N.A. lat. 2390 (Fig. 63). In the Parma Codex, fol. 16, dots mark the boundaries of the patches of color in the background (Fig. 28).

109. For multi-lobed forms, as in 2247 and 2261, cf. the Gero Codex, fol. 117 (Schardt, *Das Initial*, p. 103), Trier, Stadtbibl. 859, and Cornell University MS B 12, fol. 50v. For a parallel to the initials of 2261, cf. the Bible of Routpertus from Echternach, Gotha, Membr. 1, 1, fol. 276.

110. Cf. B.N.N.A. lat. 1496, fol. 8v(B).

CHAPTER IX

THE ORNAMENT OF THE BORDERS (FIGS. 24-27)

THE borders are an extensive repertoire of motifs each repeated in single file; one could construct from them a comprehensive treatise on Romanesque ornament, at least on the kind composed along one axis. Adapted to the narrow bands framing a picture or text, these motifs lack the freely branching forms of the ornament of the initials, which grows from inside the decorated letter and is intertwined with it. Yet under the constraints of the marginal field, this border ornament shows an unremitting search for movement and change—a great liberty of choice—not only from page to page but on the same frame. I have not seen another Romanesque manuscript with an equal variety in the borders. Most of the unit patterns are familiar from older works; but we cannot say how much of the less obvious ornament is original, since few early manuscripts of this richness have come down. One can admire, however, the painter's playful freedom of variation on certain pages and his flashes of wit in selecting a motif that corresponds to a unique design in the enclosed miniature. An adequate description of the ornament—impossible in the limited space of this study—would have to take account of the many departures from regularity even when the same unit is repeated (Figs. 26f, g, l, 27r). I have assembled on three plates (Figs. 25-27) seventy-four segments of the borders of the text which, together with the illustrations of the ornament framing the miniatures, will permit the reader to explore by himself this distinctive aspect of the book.

Every page of text is heavily framed, like the display manuscripts made for the Carolingian monarchs.[111] Except for a few pages (fols. 28v, 89v, 95) where a fourth band is added, each frame is formed of three bands of which the outer and inner are of gold and silver and the middle one is usually filled with ornament. (On twenty-four of the 220 pages it is a plain purple strip.) Fewer than twenty frames have a flat geometrical decoration of dots, circles, bars, chevrons, X's, lozenges, or arcs, some recalling inlaid gems and other jewelry designs (Figs. 12, 27 a-g). On the rest are ribbon meanders in perspective and plant forms (isolated or joined leaves, blossoms in regular alignment, a simple vine with slender or thick foliage, half palmettes or acanthus in profile—Figs. 1-3, 8, 11, 17, 20-22, 25, 26 and Colorplate 1). Among the plant forms one kind, a reduced acanthus, is usually modeled with dark lines of the pen and with shadow tones that produce an effect of the concave and convex; white calligraphic lines and dots along the edges define the contours—dots that also mark the ridges of the leaves and are sprinkled on the meanders and sometimes on a panel in a plain outer border (Fig. 27g). In many of the meanders foliage fills the widened intervals at cardinal points of the frame (Figs. 16, 18, 19). Together with the meander ribbons (on sixty-seven pages) the modeled foliate motifs (on eighty-six) are the most frequent ornament. Beside these classic types are unmodeled plant forms: vines, flat blossoms and palmettes, quatrefoils and rosettes in diapered lozenges, that recall the textile fabrics of the period (Figs. 24, 26g, h, i); there are also linear plant patterns like the goldsmith's designs in filigree and wire (Figs. 25t, 27s). On several pages the final lobe of a leaf in each turn of a rinceau is treated as a stem with knobbed lobes, as in Islamic and Byzantine art (Fig. 25q). Last should be mentioned an ornament that is specifically Northern and distinct in principle from

111. Cf. the manuscripts of Charlemagne's Court ("Ada") School: Paris, B.N.N.A. lat. 1203; Trier 22; Paris, B.N. lat. 8850; London, B. M. Harley 2788 (Wilhelm Koehler, *Die karolingischen Miniaturen*. II. *Die Hofschule*, Berlin, 1957, pls. 9ff. and passim); and the Codex Aureus of Charles the Bald, Munich, Staatsbibliothek Cim. 55 (*Der Codex Aureus der bayerischen Staatsbibliothek in München*, ed. Georg Leidinger, Munich, 1921).

In my illustrations (Figs. 25-27) all the segments are in the axis of the original, except Fig. 26a.

the other types I have listed: the compact knotted bands, intricate and of elusive continuity, which appear on eight pages (Figs. 27, i-p).

This rough inventory, disregarding the distribution, conceals an interesting fact—that there is in the choice of patterns a definite drift. While the ribbon meander and modeled acanthus—continuous repeated forms—are most frequent in the first two-thirds of the book, the artist has introduced toward the end and in particular after fol. 80 many motifs from other traditions—forms also related to metal and textile ornament—and has aligned more than a dozen different patterns on a single frame (Figs. 24, 26k, l, y), often dividing the frame into separate panels of unequal length. He has also split the ornamented band into half friezes with distinct motifs on each or run two parallel ornaments within the same band (Figs. 25w, 27f, g).

This change in the borders from the sumptuous and monumental types, the regular perspective meander and acanthus, to a less strictly coordinated form may be likened broadly to the difference between the full-page pictures with elaborate architectural settings and the smaller ones with simple grounds, set more loosely on the page. One can imagine that an old manuscript of imperial origin served the artist as a model of splendor for the large paintings and the associated ornament, while in the lesser scenes and on the pages of text he gradually freed himself from the Ottonian model and worked with forms more habitual in Burgundy. There are, indeed, striking resemblances of the first borders to the imperial manuscripts from Regensburg and their Carolingian prototypes in the Codex Aureus of Charles the Bald (Munich, Staatsbibliothek, Cim. 55). But this distinction between the foreign and native is not borne out by the choice of motifs on the frames of the pages with the smaller miniatures, or by the character of monumental decoration in Burgundy, where the acanthus and the meander were favored types.[112] More pertinent to the artist's process, I think, is the fact that the less regular ornament appears in the part of the manuscript with a long succession of pages of text between folios 45v and 102, uninterrupted by pictures. On these pages the artist, relieved of the necessity of accommodation to a painting with strongly marked vertical and horizontal axes and with large elements, human and architectural, extending through the field, and perhaps stimulated by the script with its small, discrete word-units of variable length and form which determine an irregular pattern of spacing in the parallel lines of writing, has filled the borders with many freely-chosen motifs submitted only to common requirements of compactness, of consistent color, and of a balance of accents in the frame as a whole. Here the frame is not subordinate in the same sense as on the pages with miniatures, where the decorated border adheres to the picture; on the contrary, the frame of the text is more pronounced than the writing and has a degree of independence as an object in its own right. Like the script which it encloses, the ornament of the frame invites reading as a sequence of many distinct units. One should note, however, that if this diversity of ornament in the same band is opposed in principle to the repetitive or strictly symmetrical decoration of the borders of the miniatures, and recalls the looseness of folk art in which the pattern units are treated as an array of distinct symbols, it has also a precedent in manuscripts of the Carolingian Court School,[113] where it depends perhaps on Italian art of the eighth century (like the Egino Codex). The subdivision of the frame

112. They were widely used in French mural painting of the 11th and 12th century. For early examples in and near Burgundy, cf. the remains at Les Allinges (Haute-Savoie) in P. Deschamps and M. Thibout, *La peinture murale en France*, Paris, 1951, pl. VIII; Saint-Chef (near Vienne in Dauphiné), *ibid.*, pl. X; Ternand (Rhône), *ibid.*, pp. 29ff., fig. 4; cf. also St. Pierre-les-Églises (near Chauvigny in Poitou), *ibid.*, figs. 7, 8. In my opinion, the authors date all these works too early, especially in placing St. Pierre-les-Églises, Ternand and Les Allinges in the Carolingian period.

The frequency of these widespread motifs in native mural painting (and in later monumental sculpture) does not exclude the possibility that in the Parma Codex they have been taken from a German model; it would require a more minute study of the forms to determine what features, if any, depend on the foreign source.

113. For examples, see the manuscripts of the Court school cited in note 111 above. The division of a border into units of different type is common also in Bavarian manuscripts of the 11th century; cf. the Rule of Niedermünster (G. Swarzenski, *Regensburger Malerei*, pl. II, no. 5), and Munich lat. 9476 and 6204 (Bange, *Bayerische Malerschule*, figs. 23, 25, 35-37).

into many compartments with different fillings occurs also in manuscripts of the twelfth century, especially in Italy.

Still, I do not know of a Carolingian or Ottonian manuscript with so richly varied an ornament of the borders of both miniature and text. A close relative in the tradition of sumptuous book art is the already-mentioned Codex Aureus of Charles the Bald in Munich, a French Gospels of fantastic splendor that belonged to the abbey of St. Emmeram in Regensburg and was copied there often in the tenth and eleventh centuries. But the meander, which in the Parma manuscript is so surprisingly flexible a form, varying in scale, rhythm, and filling as well as in design (Figs. 1, 3-7, 16, 27h, u), is exceptional and of meager variety in the Codex Aureus, where the foliate theme predominates; and in the superb luxuriance of his borders the Carolingian artist never attains on the pages of text the freedom and complexity of the foliate ornament of the Parma frames. Neither in the Munich manuscript nor in the works of Charlemagne's Court School, with their elaborate enclosures of the text, does a designer venture to align so many distinct motifs on a single band as in the Ildefonsus Codex. The Cluniac artist's capacity for both strict order in regular series and for a freer harmony of unique motifs with a developing variation from one to the next in color, axis and analogy of design (while maintaining some relations of symmetry), is an extraordinary phenomenon (Figs. 24, 25x, y, 26j, k, l, w, x, y); it recalls the exuberance of carved ornament on the new monumental sculpture of the time, on the capitals, archivolts, and jambs, and on the corbels and intervals of a cornice—in all of these the carving seems firmly fitted to its space, yet admits great liberty of conception in each unit even to the point of caprice. In the varying elements and rhythms of the parallel sides of the frame in the manuscript (Figs. 24, 25d, q, y; 25x, 26v; 26j, o, t) there is an effect like polyphony in multi-part music. The designer of the borders is an erudite artist who in exploiting a complex heritage of patterns is boldly imaginative, combining motifs of quite different origin and character and adapting them successfully to his lengthy strips. His impatience with the standard acanthus and meander is a sign of his inventive verve. In resolving the inevitable incongruences between pattern and field at the corners he shows much ingenuity and a quick, unpedantic hand (Figs. 25k, l, p; 26e, q; 27r).

However different in conception, the varied motifs are also brought into harmony by a common execution which is rapid, vigorous and fresh. The borders throughout are painted with the same basic palette as the initials: red, green, blue, gold and silver. The backgrounds are blue and green, the lobes of the palmettes often gold and silver. The meander is divided into planes of contrasted color, as in Carolingian and Ottonian manuscripts. On some borders the colors in the compartments are disposed in symmetrical X patterns: *abcb* on one side, *babc* on the other; but there are more complex variants of this familiar primitive form.

Most important for the effect of the enclosed paintings are the perspective meander and the modeled acanthus (and its palmette-like variants) which bring a strong plastic note to the whole page; they continue a late classic practice of salient borders that was revived by the Carolingian and Ottonian artists.[114] They are a witness to the fascination of the illusionistic—the magic of the

114. They appear in almost all the Ottonian schools. Cf. the Egbert psalter in Cividale from Reichenau (Goldschmidt, *German Illumination*, II, pl. 20); St. Gall Stiftsbibliothek 390-391 (Merton, *Die Buchmalerei in St. Gallen*, pl. 69); Paris, B.N. lat. 10501, from Trier (Goldschmidt, *op.cit.*, II, pl. 15); Darmstadt MS 1946, from Echternach; the Göttingen sacramentary from Fulda (E. H. Zimmermann, *Die Fuldaer Buchmalerei in karolingischer und ottonischer Zeit*, Halle a.S., 1910, fig. 2); Munich lat. 4456, the Sacramentary of Henry II from Regensburg (Goldschmidt, *op.cit.*, II, pls. 72ff.) and the Regensburg Pontifical of bishop Otto (1060-1089) (Swarzenski, *Regensburger Malerei*, pl. XXXII, no. 91); and manuscripts from other Bavarian centers: Munich lat. 18005, Tegernsee (Bange, *Bayerische Malerschule*, fig. 7), lat. 828 (*ibid.*, fig. 123), and Trier Domschatz cod. 140 (*ibid.*, figs. 141-143).

The insertion of acanthus at the cardinal (and sometimes other) points of the polychrome meander border, as in the Parma Codex (Figs. 16, 18, 19) occurs in the Gero Codex from Reichenau (Grabar and Nordenfalk, *Early Medieval Painting from the Fourth to the Eleventh Century*, Geneva, 1957, p. 197, colorplate) and in the Sacramentary of Henry II (Munich Clm. 4456; Goldschmidt, *op.cit.*, II, pl. 72). There is also an example in Einsiedeln MS 113, s.XI,2, enclosing an initial with the dotted trefoil (DeWald, ART BULLETIN, VII, 1925, fig. 8, pl. LVII).

seemingly tangible relief form on a flat surface—during an age of spiritualistic art. They support in the pictures the related qualities of modeling and depth, but the meander also brings out the artificial and constructed in the compositions and corresponds to elements of architecture in the scene. In its great frequency it appears more consistent with Romanesque than with Ottonian art and agrees with the monumental painting of the Burgundian region.

I have remarked before on the resemblance of the ornament of the border to the larger forms of the enclosed painting. In the first miniature (Fig. 1) the strong verticals and horizontals, the gesturing hands of the figures at the central column, and the pattern of the embracing arches, rise, bend, and turn like the bordering meander. The latter is an echo of the painting, a reduced marginal accompaniment; but it may be seen also as a nucleus from which the whole has been expanded. On Fig. 20 is another neat example of such a correspondence: the cowl and its adjoining forms resemble the close-packed triangular leaves of the frame.[115]

One should not regard the analogy of border and miniature as a set program. On only a few pages does it appear as distinctly as in the two examples that I have cited. If the verso and recto pages facing each other sometimes have a similar ornament of the two frames, as often the paired frames are different in detail, in color and in scale of elements, and even in the patterns chosen; they owe their unity to other features. Within a single frame the number of units of the same motif often differs on the two parallel sides. Clearly the painter has not aimed at a strict order, although he designs carefully with precise control of his spacing.

I must mention a particularly ingenious example of a pattern of the frame contrasted with the enclosed forms. On Fig. 22, where a large asymmetrical A is decorated with a counterclockwise spiral, the artist has superimposed a clockwise direction on the band of small foliage by alternating regular patches of light and dark, larger in scale than the single units of foliage and of marked rightward slope—creating two distinct rhythms in the same field. On the opposite page, Fig. 21, the similar plant ornament lacks that strong pulse of light and dark; less contrasted in value, it frames the image of Christ in Glory, which has a strong vertical axis.[116]

The many similarities of the details of this ornament to the foliage on the capitals and bases in the miniatures (and also to some elements in the initials) confirm the idea that the frames were designed by the Ildefonsus painter, though the execution on some pages may be credited to an assistant.[117] Many of the patterns are standard for frames in Ottonian and early Romanesque art, and we are therefore less surprised by the difference from the ornament of the initials, the lack of the latter's spiral and trefoil forms. The same separation appears in another manuscript of Cluny, Paris Bibl. Nat. lat. 1087, where the artist—very close to the style of the Ildefonsus master (and probably the same man a few years before)—has traced on a blank space at the end of a text several parallel strips of ornament (Fig. 43). Three of these bands, I have remarked before, duplicate plant motifs of the borders of the Parma Codex, while the initials correspond as faithfully to the initials of the latter (Fig. 41).[118]

115. The same pattern is found in the Codex Aureus (Leidinger, *op.cit.*, pls. 6, 8, 9), the Egbert psalter in Cividale, the Gospels of Henry IV from Regensburg (Swarzenski, *Regensburger Malerei*, pl. XXXIV); in Bavarian works (Munich lat. 6204, 12201a, Bange, *Bayerische Malerschule*, figs. 35, 81); and in manuscripts of ca. 1060 from the school of Cologne (cf. Freiburg University MS 360a, Goldschmidt, *German Illumination*, pl. 96B).

116. The sloping light-dark on fol. 45 may be seen also as a diagonal that, in paralleling the inclined Ildefonsus in the left corner of fol. 44v, helps to bind the two pages.

117. Note also that the ornamented border of fol. 102 (Fig. 23), which frames a miniature by Hand B, is like the border of Fig. 8, and that much of the ornament within the two pictures by Hand B (Fig. 23 and Colorplate 2) is similar to motifs throughout the book.

118. Cf. with the Parma Codex, fols. 18v and 19 (Fig. 25s) for the rinceaux and fol. 36 (Fig. 11) for the acanthus. The motif of the dragon biting the tail of a second beast may be compared with initials in another manuscript from Cluny, Paris, B.N.N.A. lat. 1461, fols. 1, 6, where dragons bite each other in a circle. The bands of foliate and animal ornament on this page of lat. 1087 recall a page in the Echternach Codex Aureus of Gotha-Nuremberg (Goldschmidt, *German Illumination*, II, pl. 48).

CHAPTER X

THE COLOPHON PAINTER (HAND B)

To reorient the reader after this long account of the first painter, I shall repeat some information already given at the beginning of this study.

The second hand painted two miniatures (Fig. 23 and Colorplate II) near the end of the manuscript (fols. 102, 102v) to illustrate an old colophon. It is a text that records the writing of a copy of the work of Ildefonsus by the monk Gómez of the monastery of "Abba Hildensis" at the request of Gotiscalc, bishop of Le Puy, during the latter's visit to Spain in 951. On one page the Spanish scribe is shown writing, on the other side he offers the book to the enthroned bishop. The manuscript of 951, with the original colophon, is preserved in Paris (Bibl. Nat. MS lat. 2855).[119]

It is remarkable that this colophon should not only be transcribed in the later copy of the text of Ildefonsus, but should also be illustrated, unlike the original of 951. We shall inquire later into the significance of this fact.

In the rendering of the figures the colophon painter applies faithfully the conventions of the Italo-Byzantine school of the period about 1100. His command of that style seems so complete that Georg Swarzenski could regard him as an Italian artist.[120] That first impression is strengthened by the contrast with the work of his companion painter. Yet closer study will bring out common features in the two sets of works and Hand B will appear less consistently Italian when he has been compared with other artists of the Italo-Byzantine style at Cluny. Before I go into the problem of his relation to Italian art, I shall try to describe more precisely his individual style.

What is most striking in his miniatures, when considered beside those of Hand A, is the weight of the figures, their effect of the sculptured and voluminous. Hand A's picture of Ildefonsus writing (Colorplate I) seems a flat, linear tracery beside the picture of Gómez at his desk. In the first the head-dress is a plane triangle as flat as the head it is designed to cover; the cowl of Gómez, hanging on his shoulder, is a conical vessel that could envelop the rounded mass of the head.

While no less compact and stable than A's figures, Hand B's have a greater complexity of form in neighboring details, with more contrasts of the smooth and broken, the angular and curved. His modeling and lights and division of parts are highly schematic, but he employs—at least in the figures—a more varied drawing than A's system of repeated lines. On the arms and legs the costume is divided into large cloisons by solid folds that curve broadly with the convexities of the limbs. Hand B models by light and dark—by light through white lines in a casual tracery of zigzags, triangles, meanders and comblike forms, and by dark through parallel lines drawn as folds along the contour of the limb, and sometimes through a deeper shadow tone of the local color. This combination of the graphic and the painterly in the modeling, with highlights that are complex lines spanning a surface, and with fold lines that build up a shading and rounding of the mass, is distinctive for the Italo-Byzantine style. It is in the painting of the heads, however, that the Byzantine tradition is maintained in its purest state. The grave, contemplative faces are delicately toned with red and green and brought into relief by white highlights which are applied in graded patches and blendings with the local color, or traced as slender lines along the features to form a continuous calligraphic T on the brow and nose.

The sensibility evident in the finer transitions and contrasts of light and dark appears also in the choice of colors.[121] While Hand A sets the figures on a uniform gold ground, Hand B divides

119. For the texts and their history, see above, p. 8, and below, p. 62.

120. *Salzburger Malerei*, p. 83, n. 1: "der byzantinisierende Miniator ist zweifellos ein Italiener."

121. Colorplates I and II render very well the local colors although nuances of modeling and tone, especially in the faces on fol. 102v, are lost in the reproduction.

that ground into rectangles of gold and silver—a warm and a cool metallic luminosity. In the presentation page, the order is gold and silver behind the figures, silver and gold behind the dome and towers overhead. On Fig. 23, against the gold, Hand B paints a lavender robe and a green curtain; against the silver, a blue and red desk and a light blue curtain. On the next page (Colorplate II) the bishop's robes are red and deep blue upon the silver ground.[122] Here the contrasts with cooler, more somber, and neutralized tones are more subtle than those of his fellow painter who works with bright hues.

This greater refinement of Hand B yields a less pure, less consistent effect, however, than A's best pages. In striving for richness, the colophon painter multiplies ornament and bright touches that compete with the subtler forms and colors. Where Hand A in representing a row of columns brings out the large structure by accenting the correspondences of the members in a series, painting all the columns blue and all the imposts and astragals red, B varies the colors, giving the architecture a playful, broken aspect: one column, together with its capital and astragal, is green, a second is blue, a third is purple with a purple astragal and a blue cap—all this in contrast to the sculptural, even monumental aspect of the figures. Hand A aims in his color at compactness and strength by clear contrasts of large elements or regions of the picture; Hand B enjoys scattering his contrasts and enriches every part of the field by varied details of drawing, ornament or color.

Yet B knows how to bind his elements and is fertile in coupling unlike objects through similar rhythmic lines and colors. The great ornamented dome, the towers, and the speckled entablature, accord with the bishop's elaborate costume, throne, and crozier; the rectangular arches below are like the open book. In the picture of the scribe we see the motif of the scalloped form developed progressively in the arches of the footstool, the upper edge of the writing-desk, the hanging knotted curtain, and also in the buildings on the entablature. But these objects when seen together are no eloquent group like the responding architecture in A's paintings—they have only slight expressive weight in themselves and as parts of an ensemble. The careful fitting and balance in Hand B's two miniatures are less effective perhaps because of the pronounced decoration of the major forms. The ornament of the figures, furniture, and buildings, a worldly surface decoration, stands out ineluctably in the whole which lacks the earnestness and simplicity of the best pages of the other painter. In the buildings, in particular, the details look isolated and large. In general, the architecture here contributes less to the unity of figure and setting and has little of that resonance of the humans in their surroundings which appeals to us in the strong, sober paintings by the first artist. It is as if two styles of different tendency and force of expression have been applied within the same picture and given an equal scope. But one can see already in the figures alone—and in their most Byzantine feature, the modeling with light—the distracting effect of the decorative impulse in the calligraphic caprice of the highlights. This lack of concentration, of a fully decided expression, is reflected in B's drawing of hands. They are delicate and seem diffident in grasping the book, the pen, and the crozier, compared to A's stronger, coarser hands which hold things firmly.

These qualities are not inherent in the Italo-Byzantine style as such, but arise within B's individual adaptation, which corresponds perhaps to a broader tendency of life in Cluny. When we compare Hand B with another contemporary painter of Italo-Byzantine style in Cluny, the master of the lectionary, Bibl. Nat. Nouv. Acq. lat. 2246 (Figs. 37-39, 42), B's art, accomplished as it is, seems hybrid and stiff.[123] We find in the lectionary an almost identical manner of

122. The greenish-gray patches on the figure of Gómez on fol. 102v (Colorplate II) seem to be due to the action of the binding medium of the silver background on the other side of the leaf (Fig. 23) penetrating the parchment. That is how A. P. Laurie has explained similar effects in other manuscripts (*The Pigments and Mediums of the Old Masters*, London, 1914, pp. 78, 79).

123. All the miniatures in B.N.N.A. lat. 2246 have been reproduced by Mercier, *Les primitifs français*, pls. 92-107. For a recent description of the contents of the manuscript,

drawing the heads and the same devices of lighting the brows and nose; in some respects Hand B is more authentically Byzantine—the rendering of the eyes and surrounding parts is more faithful to the Greek modeling.[124] In the miniatures of the lectionary the figures dominate the field, and the accessory elements—the architecture and furniture and the decoration of costume and borders—are not allowed to intervene in the large effect as in the colophon pictures. Where the costume is richly ornamented, as on the archangel of the Annunciation, whose robes are insignia of his heavenly office (Fig. 42), the effect is restrained and subordinate to the human actors. What inspires this painter above all are the spiritual qualities of his figures, which are realized through a suppler drawing and proportion. Beside the elongation and movement of the bodies in the lectionary, Hand B's figures look rather squat and inert. Here the religious person in his fixity has nothing of the latent emotion that we sense in the other.

Is this difference due perhaps to the constraints of the subject, the painter of the colophon having to render the static themes of the scribe and the presentation, while in the other manuscript the artist has had to imagine themes of intense feeling—Christ on the Cross and the Descent of the Holy Spirit? I do not think so, for the difference in quality that I have noted may be seen in the treatment of the common elements on the smallest scale, in the rendering of hands and single bits of drapery and especially of the highlights. There is, however, a miniature by the master of the lectionary representing a scribe, and from this work we can judge how the master approached the theme of the colophon. It is a fragment from a Bible manuscript in Montreal (Canada) and represents St. Luke writing (Fig. 50).[125] The elements of architecture and furniture, also rhythmic, reinforce the figure, prolonging its great curves and the movement of the scroll.

With all the obvious differences in their opposed richness and austerity, the two artists of the Parma Codex have common traits. Some of these point to the broadly contemporaneous in the two styles—the common heritage and outlook—others to recent contacts and exchanges between diverging schools. We are not surprised to find their works in the same book, for they share, although with varying effect, such qualities and elements as the firm colored outlines, the schematic simplicity of drawing, the layered shallow space, and the compact figures in compositions ruled by the vertical and horizontal.

A comparison of Hand B's presentation page with the first artist's painting of Ildefonsus and the Virgin (Fig. 3) will bring out this common Romanesque core. The posture of the bishop, frontal and symmetrical, corresponds to that of the enthroned Virgin, and the humble Ildefonsus is like the scribe, though one kneels and the other stands. In both works the costume is accented

see Giles Constable, "Manuscripts of Works by Peter the Venerable," in *Petrus Venerabilis 1156-1956*, edited by G. Constable and J. Kritzeck, Rome, 1956, pp. 238ff.

124. A detail that shows their close kinship as painters and perhaps their common apprenticeship, in spite of the ornamental and calligraphic treatment of the lights by B, is the identical pattern of lines on the fore-edge of books in miniatures by the two men. This is not a usual form in France, though it may be found in Italy (Fig. 51). Note, too, that the knotting of the curtain behind Gómez's head on fol. 102 is very much like the knotted end of the garment of the beardless apostle at the right of Peter in the Pentecost of 2246 (Fig. 37).

125. It is part of a leaf in the collection of Mr. L. V. Randall of Montreal, Canada, to whom I am grateful for the permission to reproduce the miniature. The text is of the argument of the Gospel of Luke. The two columns of writing, their small size (the left column is 3⅛" wide), the position of the argument (with its "explicit argumentum") and the miniature in the text, make it probable that the fragment is from a Bible rather than from a gospel or New Testament or a lectionary. A similar script appears in the Bible of Stephen Harding in Dijon (Oursel, *La miniature du XIIe siècle*, pl. XVII). The seat is like that of Gotiscalc in the Parma Codex, fol. 102v, the fore-edge of the book between the bull's feet is drawn exactly as in 2246 and Parma, fol. 102v. For a similar costume, cf. a figure in Dijon MS 641, Oursel, *op.cit.*, pl. XXXIVc. The type of evangelist with the bull at his feet occurs in an Italian Bible from Bologna, B.N. lat. 18, fol. 360v, but the bull's posture, with head turned back and looking upward, is a French Carolingian and Romanesque type (see p. 53 below); the conception of the bull as a half-figure emerging from behind Luke's seat and looking back, appears in a painting of the evangelist in a gospel manuscript of the second half of the 9th century from Innichen in the University library at Innsbruck, cod. 484 (Goldschmidt, *German Illumination*, I, pl. 52, "Alamannic"?), to which I have already referred for its background of gabled buildings, as in the Parma Codex, fol. 12v (note 53 above).

I learn from Dr. Hanns Swarzenski, on completing this study, that he had independently recognized the Cluniac origin of the leaf and knows of a related miniature of the Ascension at a dealer's in France.

by strongly marked spanning folds and the surface is illuminated by white lines, however different the patterns. And in the color, while Hand B employs the rarer tones of the Byzantine palette—the lavender and deep blue—their somberness and delicacy are set beside sharp notes of red and bright blue which are dominants in his companion's pictures.

There are more specific traces of Hand A's art in Hand B. Not only does B accept the type of border used by A; he applies its elements to the miniature itself, painting the same band of foliage on the frame of the first picture and on the base of the towers in the second. In dividing the border of the second miniature into alternate silver and gold strips that correspond to the division of the background of the enclosed scene, he exploits a treatment of the frame that occurs elsewhere in the book (e.g., fols. 99v, 100).[126] Like the Ildefonsus painter, Hand B sets his figures in an architecture that combines interior and exterior views, and attaches the boundaries of the building to the inner border. If the contact is less strict in the picture of the scribe (Fig. 23), it is because the curtain projects outside the columns and there is no upper border; but curtain and bases do touch the other borders.[127] Both painters give their domes a decoration of gored or petaled forms, radiating from a knob.

From these relations to Hand A we may conclude that Hand B assimilated the Italo-Byzantine features after having learned to paint in the native manner with its Germanic elements.[128] The same process is observable in German art in Regensburg, Salzburg, and elsewhere in Bavaria in the second half of the eleventh century;[129] the German monastic artists applied Byzantine forms to figures of traditional Ottonian art with a German setting, while maintaining also the German ornament and style of initial.

There are, of course, Italian details in B's architecture, but it is not always easy to say whether an Italian element has come from Italy directly or belongs to a stratum of Italian forms in older Northern art. An example is the stilted lintel in the presentation page (Colorplate II), that appears also in several of A's miniatures (Colorplate I and Fig. 4). This form, I have remarked earlier, was known in Italy before and during the Carolingian period, but was widely diffused in the North and undoubtedly owes its presence in Hand A's work to the Carolingian-Ottonian tradition.[130] Yet in B's painting the slight curvature of this lintel is perhaps a reflection of recent Italian models.[131] And several accompanying details of classical form seem to confirm the Italian origin. The leaves of Hand B's capitals are curly and modeled in the ancient manner, and the columns are enriched by flutings and in one case by a surface ornament that vaguely simulates a marble grain. The egg and dart—again a classical motif—is applied to the

126. The division of the background into four rectangles, with diagonal symmetry of the two colors, may be a Northern feature. It occurs in the Bamberg Apocalypse from Reichenau, but with gold and lilac as the paired colors (H. Wölfflin, *Die Bamberger Apokalypse, Eine Reichenauer Bildhandschrift vom Jahre 1000*, Munich, 1921, pl. 27.

127. The curtains behind the scribe, knotted around the columns, are a feature of Ottonian and later German evangelist-portraits (cf. Munich, lat. 4454, from Reichenau; 18005, Tegernsee, Bange, *Bayerische Malerschule*, figs. 8-10; 9476, *ibid.*, figs. 21-23, 25; Fulda Landesbibl., Cod. A.a.44, *ibid.*, fig. 27). The central dome between two towers over an entablature is also found in Bavarian manuscripts of the 11th century: Munich lat. 6204 (*ibid.*, fig. 36), 18005 (*ibid.*, fig. 7), 12201a (*ibid.*, figs. 81, 82). The quatrefoils of the entablature decorate the border of the painting of the Last Judgment at Burgfelden (Paul Weber, *Die Wandgemälde zu Burgfelden*, Darmstadt, 1896, pl. I).

128. I must admit, however, the possibility that the colophon painter, having first learned to paint from an Italian artist at Cluny, adopted elements of Hand A and of the prevailing Germanic tradition to accommodate his own manner to the ornament and general aspect of the book.

129. Cf. Pierpont Morgan Library MS 780, the pericope book of Master Bertolt from Salzburg (ca. 1070), Swarzenski, *Regensburger Malerei*, pl. XXVIII; the Gospels of Henry IV from Regensburg, *ibid.*, pls. XXXIII; Fulda, Landesbibliothek Cod. A.a.44, Bange, *Bayerische Malerschule*, figs. 27, 28 (possibly West German); Trier, Domschatz cod. 140, *ibid.*, figs. 141-143, a good parallel to the Parma Codex.

130. See above, p. 22 and n. 56.

131. Like the frescoes of the life of Saint Alexis at S. Clemente in Rome, and of Tuscania (see the following note for the references). Cf. also the drawing in Monte Cassino, cod. 99, Fig. 51. The curved form appears already in the ninth century on the gold altar of S. Ambrogio in Milan. It is from a North Italian model that the painter of the Poussay gospels (Paris, B.N. lat. 10514) from Reichenau probably derived the curved stilted lintel (Sauerland and Haseloff, *Der Psalter Erzbischof Egberts*, pl. 55). The same form occurs early in the 11th century on the gold altar frontal of Aachen Cathedral (attributed to Fulda and Mainz) in the scenes of the Last Supper and the Washing of Feet (Schnitzler, *Rheinische Schatzkammer*, pls. 79, 80).

entablature above the writing monk and on the cornice of the right tower on the next page.[132] Symptomatic, too, is the conception of the astragal, which on two columns is a thickening of the shaft; for the other painter it is always a separate member, framing the capital like the abacus or impost and appearing as a molding of the lower edge of the capital. The latter is the normal practice of the Romanesque builders and stone-carvers, in keeping with their preference for the inert, wall-like pier as a supporting member; the astragal as a molding of the thickened upper end of the column is the more organic and plastic classical form. But this form survived (or was revived) in the twelfth century in French as well as Italian schools that show in other respects an awareness of ancient art.[133] In Cluny the famous capitals of the choir, which impress one by their wonderfully fresh modeling of the classic acanthus, are carved like ancient Roman capitals without astragals. And elsewhere in Burgundian buildings may be found the egg-and-dart and the fluted columns and pilasters.[134] It may be that the introduction of classical forms from Italy through the painters in the late eleventh century stimulated the builders and sculptors in Burgundy to study and adopt elements of Roman art still visible in ancient remains in France.

But Hand B is not at all consistent in his use of these classic forms and betrays a restless hybrid taste in varying his architectural details. If the column at the right has a Roman astragal, the other two are plainly medieval, one with two equal moldings at the top, the other with a square block.[135] The double astragal is found especially in Ottonian art, in Trier and Echternach: in Trier with a thicker and a lighter member,[136] in Echternach with equal moldings as in Cluny.[137] The Trier painting of Pope Gregory in the famous Registrum Gregorii—a refined and masterly work—retains far more of classic feeling for the atmospheric and plastic; compare in particular the modeled pallium of the Saint, responding to the folds of the costume and body beneath, with the rigidly flat form in Parma. Yet in the latter the capitals, which appear to follow Ottonian models, are drawn with curled acanthus ending in a crocket as in advanced Romanesque and early Gothic buildings; while the master of the Trier painting draws the acanthus in flattened profile (Fig. 68).[138]

The conception of the scribe presenting the book to the bishop is also probably of Northern origin. The scribe in profile holding the book, the bishop enthroned frontally at the right, had appeared for nearly three hundred years in the numerous copies of the presentation miniature of Rabanus Maurus' *De Laudibus Sanctae Crucis*, originally a Fulda work of the early ninth century.[139] The same type, sometimes with bishop (or abbot) and patron saint as donor and recipient, is found nearer to the Cluny manuscript in time and place in the presentation page of

132. Cf. the Italian examples at S. Pudenziana, Rome (W. Paeseler, "Die römische Weltgerichtstafel im Vatikan," *Kunstgeschichtliches Jahrbuch der Bibliothek Hertziana*, II, 1938, fig. 316); the painted wooden panel of the Last Judgment in the Vatican (*ibid.*, fig. 277); a fresco in the crypt at Aquileia (Mercier, *Les primitifs français*, pl. 58); the fresco of the Birth of St. John at S. Pietro in Tuscania (Ch.-A. Isermeyer, "Die mittelalterlichen Malereien der Kirche S. Pietro in Tuscania," *Kunstgeschichtliches Jahrbuch der Bibliothek Hertziana*, II, 1938, fig. 258); a fresco from Magliano Romano, now in the Galleria Nazionale in Rome (E. B. Garrison, *Studies in the History of Mediaeval Italian Painting*, III, Florence, 1958, fig. 243); S. Clemente, Rome, frescoes of the lower church; Rome, Bibl. Vallicelliana MS E. 16, evangeliary, Rome, early 12th century (*ibid.*, fig. 229); Monte Cassino, MS 99 (Fig. 51); Naples, Bibl. Naz. codex VIII.C.4, Beneventan (G. Ladner, "Die italienische Malerei im 11. Jahrhundert," *Jahrbuch der kunsthistorischen Sammlungen in Wien*, N.F.V., 1931, fig. 19).

133. For Italian examples, cf. S. Pudenziana, the Vatican panel of the last Judgment, the Vallicelliana MS E. 16, and Monte Cassino MS 99, all cited in the preceding note.

134. For the egg-and-dart, see Porter, *Romanesque Sculpture*, ill. 84 (Perrecy-les-Forges, Saône-et-Loire, archivolt), 93 (Neuilly-en-Donjon, Allier, tympanum), and Berzé-la-Ville, archivolt in fresco of St. Blaise (Mercier, *Les primitifs français*, pl. 23). The fluted columns and pilasters appear in Burgundy at Autun, Cluny, Avallon and elsewhere.

135. The square block appears between capital and column in a fresco at S. Pudenziana, Rome, as a kind of pseudo-Ionic element (Paeseler, *Jahrbuch der Bibliothek Hertziana*, II, 1938, fig. 316), anticipated already in the painting of the Annunciation at S. Urbano alla Caffarella (Ladner, *Jahrbuch der kunsthistorischen Sammlungen in Wien*, 1931, fig. 72).

136. Cf. the Registrum Gregorii, miniature of Pope Gregory, Goldschmidt, *German Illumination*, II, pl. 7.

137. Goldschmidt, *German Illumination*, II, pl. 44. But see also Einsiedeln Stiftsbibliothek MS 151, s.XI.2 (DeWald, ART BULLETIN, VII, 1925, fig. 27) for the double astragal.

138. In Monte Cassino MS 99, fol. 5 (Annunciation), the more Byzantine hand draws capitals with curled leaves, but they are as a whole less classic in form than those of the Parma colophon painter or the Registrum Gregorii. See Janine Wettstein, *Sant'Angelo in Formis et la peinture médiévale en Campanie*, Geneva, 1960, pl. 23, and Peter Baldass, "Disegni

the Egbert psalter in Cividale,[140] written in Reichenau in the late tenth century, and in works from Echternach and St. Gall.[141] Significant, too, in the Parma image is its place at the end of the text of Ildefonsus, where the colophon had been transferred from its position at the beginning of the book in the Le Puy copy. In the great Carolingian Bible of Charles the Bald, it is at the end that the monks of Tours are represented offering the book to the monarch;[142] and this Northern custom is maintained in the display manuscripts made for the German emperors at Echternach in the eleventh century.[143] Some decades after the Parma Codex was illustrated, a painter at Cluny decorated the famous catalogue of the library of the abbey with a miniature at the end, showing a monk offering the catalogue to the abbot Hugo III (1158-1161).[144]

There is, however, in an earlier Italian manuscript an arresting parallel to the Cluny painting. It is a drawing of the presentation of a book to Saint Benedict in a homiliary of Monte Cassino (MS 99) written in 1072 (Fig. 51).[145] The resemblance is not only in the broad conception of the subject, with the standing monk at one side and the seated Benedict at the right; several features of drawing and ornament, too, recall the Cluny miniature. In the architectural setting are the rectangular opening, the fluted and marbled columns with the astragal drawn as part of the column in the classical manner, and the egg-and-dart ornament.[146] In the figures the draped surface of the lap and legs is divided into close-fitting, almond-shaped units and with these occur the nested V folds and the long parallel lines that shade and model the lower edge of the sleeve and the back, as in the Cluny figures.

In discussing the history of the Rabanus presentation type, Prochno has conjectured that an image of Saint Benedict giving the rule to Maurus in a supposed Monte Cassino manuscript of

della Scuola Cassinense del Tempo di Desiderio," *Bollettino d'Arte*, XXXVII, 1952, pp. 102-114, fig. 15.

139. See Prochno, *Das Schreiber- und Dedikationsbild*, I, pls. 11ff. and pp. xxiii and 16. A copy of the Rabanus text is listed in the 12th-century catalogue of the Cluny library; see Delisle, *Fonds de Cluni*, Paris, 1884, p. 358, no. 345 ("mirabile opus ejus de laude crucis").

140. Prochno, *Das Schreiber- und Dedikationsbild*, pl. 32. Cf. also the presentation page of the Codex Egberti (Trier MS 24) and the Gero Codex in Darmstadt (*ibid.*, pl. 28). Interesting for the Parma manuscript is the miniature of a scribe sitting beside the frontal Jerome in a tall and elaborate architectural setting in the gospel book in the Cologne Priesterseminar, H. Ehl, *Die ottonische Kölner Buchmalerei*, Bonn-Leipzig, 1922, fig. 63.

141. St. Gall, Stiftsbibliothek 390 (the Hartker antiphonary, 986-1017, Prochno, *Das Schreiber- und Dedikationsbild*, pl. 21). Cf. also London, B.M. Harley MS 2908, from Augsburg (?), *ibid.*, pl. 40. The frontispiece with scribe and seated frontal bishop appears in manuscripts of Einsiedeln in the 10th and 11th century, see DeWald, ART BULLETIN, VII, 1925, fig. 33 (MS 167), fig. 31 (MS 156).

For Echternach cf. Paris, B.N.N.A. lat. 2196, evangeliary, ca. 1040, abbot Gerhard of Luxeuil presenting the book to St. Peter against a background of arches (Prochno, pl. 48); Bremen, Stadtbibliothek, MS b. 21 (1039-1043), pericope of Henry III, *ibid.*, pls. 49, 50; Gotha, Landesbibliothek MS I. 70, ca. 1100, *ibid.*, pl. 55. I note here that the types of Gómez writing and of the frontal seated bishop correspond to portraits of Matthew and Mark (in episcopal dress) in manuscripts of Trier and Echternach (Paris, B.N. lat. 8851, the Gospels of the Ste. Chapelle, Sauerland and Haseloff, *Der Psalter Erzbischof Egberts*, pl. 50; the Gotha Codex Aureus, Goldschmidt, *German Illumination*, II, pl. 44).

142. W. Koehler, *Die karolingischen Miniaturen*, I, *Die Schule von Tours*, Berlin, 1930, pl. 76 (fol. 423).

143. As in the Bremen pericope book of Henry III, fols. 125v, 126 (Prochno, *Das Schreiber- und Dedikationsbild*, pls. 49, 50, and Goldschmidt, *German Illumination*, II, pl. 52). Cf. also Valenciennes, Bibl. mun. MS 502, fol. 74, Vita Sancti Amandi by Milo, a later 11th-century copy of a manuscript of 845-855: a monk gives the book to the enthroned Charles the Bald, under an arch with spandrel towers (Schramm, *Die deutschen Kaiser und Könige*, fig. 30, and I, p. 179).

The example of a presentation picture at or near the end of a book in a South Italian work of the 13th century, the Manfred Bible (Vatican, lat. 36, fol. 522v), was perhaps inspired by a Northern model. See Graf zu Erbach-Fürstenau, *Die Manfredbibel*, Leipzig, 1910, pl. I, and pp. 36ff. There are several examples of self-portraits of scribes in the colophons at the end of Italian manuscripts: an evangeliary in Padua (B. Katterbach, *Le Miniature dell' evangeliario di Padova dell' anno 1170*, Vatican City, 1931, pls. B and XXII) and the epistolary of 1259 in the same city (B. Katterbach, *Le Miniature dell' epistolario di Padova dell' anno 1259*, Vatican City, 1932, pl. XLVI).

144. The original has been lost, but it is described in a manuscript of the 17th century, Delisle, *Fonds de Cluni*, p. 337. The description is worth quoting for its suggestion of resemblance to the Parma miniature: "Vetus catalogus bibliothecae Cluniacensis tempore Hugonis abbatis factus, ut ex ejus imagine in ultima pagina repraesentata liquet; ibi videre est tam ipsum Hugonem abbatem quam monachum offerentem illi librum, cum cuculla strictarum manicarum et acuminati et angusti colobii seu caputii repraesentatos manifestissime."

145. The abbot Desiderius, with square nimbus, introduces the donor, John, to Saint Benedict; at the latter's feet kneels the scribe, Leo. I wish to thank Dr. Janine Wettstein of Geneva for the kind loan of her photograph and her permission to reproduce it. She has discussed this drawing in her dissertation (*Sant'Angelo in Formis*, pp. 116ff.). See also P. Baldass, *Bollettino d'Arte*, XXXVII, 1952, and Herbert Bloch's important study in *Dumbarton Oaks Papers*, III, 1946, p. 202.

146. On the astragal and the egg-and-dart ornament, see page 37 above. This ornament alone, which is so common in Italian painting of the period, is enough, I believe, to throw doubt on de Francovich's view that the Byzantine current in France is entirely independent of Italian art. See his article "Problemi della pittura e della scultura preromanica," *Set-*

the eighth century was the model of the first Rabanus miniature.[147] But the examples which are preserved in manuscripts of the Rule of Saint Benedict from the post-Carolingian period are not as close to the Parma miniature as are the presentation figures of the Rabanus scene and the later German works that I have cited.[148] If the colophon master found his model in Italian art, it was a work already influenced by the Carolingian and Ottonian type.[149]

To distinguish the Italian and the Germanic-Burgundian in this manuscript of Cluny is therefore more difficult than at first appears. In Monte Cassino, too, there was, as in Cluny, a connection with Ottonian art. The Emperor, Henry II, presented to the Italian abbey a richly ornamented book, made in Regensburg and now in the Vatican Library (Ottob. lat. 74), with miniatures in which I have noted similarities to the work of the Ildefonsus painter.[150] The initial ornament of Monte Cassino in the eleventh century, unique as it is, owes much to Northern art in its animal, foliate, and interlace forms.[151]

timane di Studio del Centro Italiano di studi sull'alto medioevo, II (Spoleto, April 6-13, 1954), Spoleto, 1955, pp. 507ff., 516, 517.

147. *Das Schreiber- und Dedikationsbild*, pp. 16 and xxiii. For an early Italian example of a similar theme, cf. the miniature in the 9th-century Codex Juvenianus in the Biblioteca Vallicelliana in Rome; the scribe at the right offers the book to the elevated enthroned Saint Lawrence at the left (J. Braun, *Die liturgische Gewandung*, Freiburg i.Br., 1907, fig. 125).

148. For other examples of presentation in Monte Cassino, cf. Cassinensis 175 (915-934) and 73 (1022-1032), Bloch, *Dumbarton Oaks Papers*, III, 1946, figs. 217, 218, abbots offering books to Saint Benedict. If in the Monte Cassino miniatures, the receiving figure is in three-quarters view and asymmetrical, there are parallels to the frontally enthroned Gotiscalc of the Parma Codex in manuscripts of the Roman school, e.g., Vatican lat. 6074 (Garrison, *Studies*, I, p. 79, fig. 105); St. Nicholas' crozier with foliate spiral end is like Gotiscalc's.

149. See page 38 above and notes 139-143.

150. See pages 21, 22 above and notes 14, 50, 51, 62 and 75. On the presentation to Monte Cassino and the political context, see Herbert Bloch, *Dumbarton Oaks Papers*, III, 1946, pp. 177ff.

151. See F. von Baldass, "Zur Initialornamentik der süditalienischen Nationalschrift," *Anzeiger der philos.-hist. Klasse der kais. Akademie der Wissenschaften*, Wien, XLVIII, 1911, pp. 290-298, and Bloch, *Dumbarton Oaks Papers*, III, 1946, pp. 202ff.

CHAPTER XI

CLUNY AND THE ITALO-BYZANTINE STYLE

THE Italo-Byzantine style in Cluny—in fact the whole broad Byzantinizing current in Romanesque art—has been referred by several writers to the influence of the Monte Cassino school. Earlier than any of the Romanesque examples elsewhere is a manuscript of Monte Cassino, Vatican lat. 1202, with pictures of the Life of Saint Benedict (Fig. 56), written in the early 1070's by the same scribe as Casinensis 99.[152] In its many painted illustrations the typical *cloisonné* divisions of the garment on the legs and arms are more pronounced than in the other book; almond-shaped, triangular and near-circular, they are modeled by patterned angular white lines as in the Parma colophon pictures. Here we see also another of the latter's forms: the hem folded to show alternately its inner and outer sides. The posture of Gómez—so monastic in feeling, with feet close together and with body bent at the waist and head—is a common stance in the Monte Cassino manuscript.

In neither of these Italian books is there, however, a completely painted picture in the Romanesque or Ottonian sense; the Byzantine figure types are brought together on an empty ground in a loosely contrived setting, which is often unframed.[153] In this school, for a closed image with great expressive force one must turn to the stupendous frescoes of Sant'Angelo in Formis, where the new Byzantine forms seem to have been fused with a strong native Campanian art. But this native art was probably an outgrowth of an earlier phase for which an older Byzantine style, brought to Italy in the preceding centuries, had supplied the basic forms, as in the frescoes of Castelseprio and Volturno and later in the Exultet Rolls.[154] What is preserved in Monte Cassino from the last third of the eleventh century (admitting the incompleteness of a description limited to the miniatures, for the lost wallpaintings might have given us another view of the whole) depends on a development within Byzantine art since the end of the tenth century that was transmitted to other Western centers as well.[155] The *cloisonné* forms of drapery and the modeling by geometrically patterned highlights are established features in the Menologion of Basil II (Vatican Greek MS 1613)[156] and in the mosaics of St. Luke at Phocis, a more provincial Greek work.[157] Even what appears to be a stylized, reductive Western treatment of the subtler Byzantine forms can be matched in Greek manuscripts of the eleventh and twelfth centuries.[158] The line between

152. The miniatures have been reproduced by M. Inguanez and M. Avery, *Miniature Cassinesi del secolo XI illustranti la vita di S. Benedetto*, Monte Cassino, 1934. They were perhaps copied from the gold antependium with scenes from the life of St. Benedict ordered by Desiderius in Constantinople about 1068: Bloch, *Dumbarton Oaks Papers*, III, 1946, p. 201.

153. In the presentation miniature, Fig. 56, the superposed arcaded buildings behind Benedict suggest an influence from Vatican Ottob. lat. 74.

154. It is this earlier art of Monte Cassino and the Beneventan school that was reproduced in several drawings in a manuscript of the lives of saints, written at St. Martial in Limoges about 1000–Paris, B.N. lat. 5301–as we can judge not only from the figure style but also from the associated intrusive ornament of one of the initials (Q, 300v) with contorted, excited beasts; cf. fols. 196, 236v, 279v (Thomas) and 300v (the Matthew symbol) with Vatican lat. 9820 (Exultet Roll from Volturno) and Rome, Casanatense 724 B.I.13, both of the 10th century (Myrtilla Avery, *The Exultet Rolls of Southern Italy*, Princeton, 1936, II, pls. CXLII, CXLVI, CXII). Jean Porcher has derived these drawings of Limoges from a Byzantine work such as the Peter on the ivory cover of the gradual of Henry II in the Bamberg library; see his article "Les ivoires byzantins et l'enluminure limousine à la fin du Xe siècle," *Neue Beiträge zur Geschichte des I. Jahrtausends* (*Spätantike und Byzanz, Forschungen zur Kunstgeschichte und christlichen Archäologie*, I, 1, 1951, pp. 189-190, figs. 51, 52) and his remarks in *Byzance et la France Médiévale, Manuscrits à Peintures du IIe au XVIe siècle*. Bibliothèque Nationale, Paris, 1958, p. 62, no. 110.

155. The transmission has been studied by W. Koehler, "Byzantine Art in the West," *Dumbarton Oaks Inaugural Lectures, 1940*, Cambridge, Mass., 1941, pp. 61-87; Garrison, *Studies*, III, pp. 206, 207; and Otto Pächt, in Pächt, Dodwell, and Wormald, *The St. Albans Psalter*, pp. 122-125, pl. 143.

156. For its date, 979-984, see S. Der Nersessian, "Remarks on the Dating of the Menologion and Psalter of Basil II," *Byzantion*, XV, 1940-41, pp. 104ff. The cloisonné system is already apparent in some figures in Paris, B.N. gr. 510, dated 867-886 (cf. fol. 75, the Transfiguration, D. T. Rice, *The Art of Byzantium*, New York, 1959, pl. 85).

157. E. Diez and O. Demus, *Byzantine Mosaics in Greece. Hosios Lucas and Daphni*, Cambridge, Mass., 1931. See also the lesser known frescoes of the crypt: O. Morisani, "Gli Affreschi dell' Hosios Lukas in Focide," *Critica d'Arte*, IX, 1962, pp. 1-17. To the same current, related to Italo-Byzantine art, belong the frescoes of St. Sophia at Ochrid in Western Macedonia.

158. Cf. the lectionary in the Pierpont Morgan Library,

the Byzantine and the Western is therefore unclear; at least it is not as distinct as is often supposed.

One should note, too, that the new current in Byzantine art, which was the source of the Western forms that we are considering, was not the only Byzantine manner in the eleventh century. Another style, more voluminous and classical in form, was practiced at the same time (it may be found in some pages of the Menologion of Basil II)[159] and was also imitated in the West, as in certain manuscripts of Regensburg in the first half of the eleventh century,[160] though with little effect on the general trend of contemporary Western art.

As early as 1066 the abbot Desiderius (1057-1087) of Monte Cassino, later Pope Victor III, had begun to import artists and works of art from Constantinople for his great enterprise of rebuilding and decorating the abbey church, and incited the young artist-monks to learn from the Greek masters. In assimilating the noble foreign style, the native artists schematized further the canonic formulas of drawing, modeling and lighting, and reduced their subtleties to more obvious and sometimes more forceful shapes and contrasts. But they retained the aristocratic slenderness of the Greek figures even in the monastic types.

During the second half of the eleventh century other Western centers beside Monte Cassino received the new Byzantine art. In Germany the Greek forms seem to have reached the Bavarian and Rhenish schools directly from the East or possibly from Venice. In 1070 the monks of S. Paolo fuori le mura in Rome, whose abbey had been reformed by Cluny, obtained from Constantinople bronze doors with figures in Byzantine style.[161] And toward 1100 the frescoes of the underground church of San Clemente in Rome show a masterful handling of Greek forms in a local style of great elegance, with beautiful silhouettes and surface pattern and a new power of representing the contemporary ecclesiastical scene in its ceremonial and festive aspect. In slightly later paintings in Santa Pudenziana in Rome and at Nepi and in Roman manuscripts,[162] the recently imported Byzantine drapery forms are translated into large rhythmical linear schemes around a kernel space, which become standard for this phase of Romanesque art throughout Western Europe. The appearance of related versions of the Italo-Byzantine style in widely separated Western centers around 1100—in the Stavelot Bible of 1097, in the frescoes of Saint-Savin, in the Cluny lectionary and the Ildefonsus Codex, in manuscripts of Angers, Limoges, Dijon, and some German schools—requires that we consider the practice of this art in Cluny not so much as the outcome of a unique influence from Monte Cassino, but as part of a broader European movement resuming an older attraction to the superior Byzantine art. We may assume that Cluny was important in promoting this style in France. That both Rome and Cluny owe these forms to Monte Cassino is impossible to say at present with certainty; the disappearance of the frescoes of the church built by Desiderius has deprived us of the most essential evidence. Given the close ties of Rome and Monte Cassino, is it not more reasonable to describe their styles as variants of a single Roman-Campanian art, resting on a common culture and the renewed economic and political relations with Byzantium in the course of the eleventh century? With its growing strength the Roman clergy found in Byzantine art an appealing visual expression of its own ideals of authority, nobility, and spiritual power. For Cluny, at any rate, Monte Cassino during this period was less

MS 692 (*Catalogue of the Exhibition of Illuminated Manuscripts*, New York, 1934, pl. 36) and the Vienna National Library MS Suppl. gr. 164, dated 1109.

159. *Il Menologio di Basilio II* (*Codice Vaticano greco 1613*), Torino, 1907, pls. 50, 61, 365, and *passim*.

160. Cf. Munich lat. 4456, the Sacramentary of Henry II (1002-1014), Goldschmidt, *German Illumination*, II, pls. 72-75, and Swarzenski, *Regensburger Buchmalerei*, pls. VII, VIII, especially the modeling of the head and hands of Gregory, and the figure of Christ in the mandorla. There was also a strong Byzantinizing trend in the manuscripts of Cologne and Mainz in the early 11th century. See Nordenfalk and Grabar, *Early Medieval Painting*, p. 208.

161. See Th. Preston, Jr. *The Bronze Doors of Monte Cassino and St. Paul's*, Rome, Princeton, 1915. The abbot of S. Paolo f.l.m. in 1070 was Hugo's friend, Hildebrand, ho had visited Constantinople that year and was later to become Pope Gregory VII.

162. Cf. Rome, Bibl. Vallicelliana MS E.16 (Garrison, *Studies*, III, figs. 226-229); Vatican, Barberini lat. 587 (Sta. Cecilia Bible), *ibid.*, III, 1, fig. 11; Florence, Bibl. Laur. Pl. 17.27, an evangeliary from S. Cecilia, Rome, *ibid.*, fig. 10, p. 18, and II, fig. 22, and the Vatican panel of the Last Judgment (see note 132 above).

significant than Rome, to which Cluny was subject and from which it received exemption from local episcopal control. Cluny's increasingly centralized order and European outlook in the second half of the century perhaps made her more receptive to the Byzantine style. In the eleventh century Cluny's aims were supported by the popes, who shared with Cluny the conception of a disciplined church under a single head and independent of secular control. The period of adoption of the Italo-Byzantine style in Cluny coincides with the rule of Pope Urban II (1088-1099), a former prior of Cluny.

The painting of the Pentecost (Fig. 37) in the lectionary (Bibl. Nat. Nouv. Acq. lat. 2246) is a revealing document of Cluny's Roman outlook. Christ and Peter are united by a common central axis, a conception unusual in the picturing of the subject before this time.[163] In Byzantine art Christ does not appear in images of the Pentecost, nor is Peter singled out among the apostles through a favored position.[164] In the West, where Peter is often central, Christ is generally absent in this scene;[165] and where He does appear, as in the Drogo Sacramentary, Peter is off-center.[166] The formation of the Cluniac image may be reconstructed from a few surviving works as an original synthesis of Italian and Northern types. On an ivory box made for Monte Cassino in 1071 or 1072, which later came to the abbey of Farfa, a house near Rome that had been reformed by Cluny, the Pentecost, like the accompanying scenes of the life of Christ, is Byzantine in some details; but the enthroned Christ is set above the heads of the apostles and the dove descends from a hand beneath his feet.[167] The same type, with Christ in a medallion, is found on an icon in the monastery of Mount Sinai; it has been attributed by its recent editor to Palestinian art of the seventh century, a monastic tradition independent of the Byzantine.[168] In Cluny this conception was fused with another that had arisen in France in the ninth century. The miniature of the Pentecost in the Drogo Sacramentary shows Christ above the apostles, with the rays and the dove issuing from his hand as well as from the isolated hand of God the Father, undoubtedly to affirm the "filioque" of the Western doctrine of the procession of the Holy Spirit, which divided the Latin from the Greek church.[169] In later art, this counter-Byzantine aim has disappeared and Christ alone is represented as the source of the rays.[170] The synthesis of the Carolingian and the Palestinian-Italian monastic types, with a dominant Peter, is probably the work of Cluny; it culminates in the grandiose tympanum of Vézelay, where Peter is subordinated. In the lectionary miniature the conception of Christ—a bust with extended arms—is like that of God in Creation scenes in Italian art.[171]

163. On the iconography of the Pentecost see L. Réau, *L'iconographie de l'art chrétien*, II, 2, Paris, 1957, pp. 591ff., with bibliography, a disappointingly meager account. The dissertation of Stephan Seeliger, *Die Ikonographie des Pfingstwunders*, Munich, 1956, has not been available to me.

164. For the Pentecost in Byzantine art, see A. Grabar, "Le schéma iconographique de la Pentecôte," *Recueil d'Études*, Seminarium Kondakovianum, Prague, 1928.

165. Cf. A. Goldschmidt, *Die Elfenbeinskulpturen*, I, Berlin, 1914, no. 27 ("Ada" school); St. Gall, Stiftsbibliothek MSS 338, 340, 341, Merton, *Die Buchmalerei in St. Gallen*, pls. 80, 81; the Nuremberg-Gotha Codex Aureus from Echternach, Metz, *Das goldene Evangelienbuch*, pl. 86; the Egbert Codex, Trier MS 24, fol. 103; etc.

166. Boinet, *La miniature carolingienne*, Paris, 1913, pl. 88. In the sacramentary of the Cathedral of Limoges, Paris, B.N. lat. 9438, fol. 87, there is no apostle directly below Christ; see *L'art roman à Saint-Martial de Limoges*, Catalogue de l'Exposition, Limoges, 1950, pl. XXII.

167. See H. Bloch, *Dumbarton Oaks Papers*, III, 1946, pp. 208ff. and fig. 252. There is no central apostle here; the apostles are divided in two separate groups, as later in the Limoges manuscript, Paris, B.N. lat. 9438.

168. G. and M. Sotiriou, *Eikones tes Mones Sina*, Athens, 1958, figs. 17, 19, pp. 34, 35. This icon reflects a type known through one of the Monza ampullae, with an enthroned Christ, a hand, rays, dove, and standing apostles and Virgin.

169. This doctrine may account for the two phials in the beak of the dove in the Baptism scene in the Benedictional of St. Ethelwold (975-980); Grabar and Nordenfalk, *Early Medieval Painting*, p. 180.

170. For other examples of Christ as the source in the Pentecost, cf. the Sacramentary of Limoges, Paris, B.N. lat. 9438 (cited in note 166 above); the manuscript of the New Testament from Verona (13th cent.), Vatican lat. 39 (*Gazette des Beaux-Arts*, LXV, 1923, vol. 2, p. 37); and a manuscript from St. Trond (E. G. Millar, *The Library of A. Chester Beatty, A Descriptive Catalogue of the Western Manuscripts*, Oxford, 1927, I, pl. 68c).

171. Cf. the lost Roman fresco reproduced by Wilpert from an old drawing in the Vatican library (*Die römischen Mosaiken und Malereien*, Freiburg i.Br., 1916, II, p. 597, fig. 241) and the mosaic in Monreale (O. Demus, *The Mosaics of Norman Sicily*, London, 1949, fig. 93). Other examples are in the Bible of St. Vaast, Boulogne, Bibl. Mun. MS 5, fol. 1; Moulins, Bible of Souvigny, fol. 4v; Bible in the John Rylands Library, Manchester (R. Fawtier, *La Bible historiée tout figurée de la John Rylands Library*, pl. 45A). There is a simi-

The inscription on the band across his arms, "Ecce ego mitto promissum patris mei in vos," from Luke 24:49, has suggested to scholars that the scene is not a Descent of the Holy Spirit but rather Christ Appearing to the Apostles after his resurrection and promising the future Pentecostal descent of the Spirit, as described by Luke.[172] The prominent rays and other features make that interpretation improbable. The position of Christ does not agree with the account in Luke: "Jesus himself stood in the midst of them. . . . He showed them his hands and his feet" (24:36, 40). The rendering of the bust of Christ in a medallion *above* the sitting apostles is hardly a medieval way of representing Christ appearing among the apostles. It conveys rather the transcendence of Christ, his heavenly position, with respect to the event on earth, as in a miniature in a Lombard manuscript of the thirteenth century (Vatican, lat. 39) where Christ is enthroned in a mandorla above the apostles who receive the rays as in the Cluny lectionary.[173] On a side door at Vézelay the scene of Christ's appearance among the apostles after the Resurrection shows Christ standing among them, as we would expect.[174] In the Cluny lectionary the gesture of Peter pointing to his book alludes, I believe, to his long speech on the occasion of the descent of the Holy Spirit, reported in Acts 2, in which he refers to the gift of tongues by the Holy Spirit as the fulfillment of a prophecy of Joel.[175] In reply to the mockers, "Peter lifted up his voice and said to them: This is what was spoken by the prophet Joel: And it shall come to pass in the last days, says God, I will pour out of my spirit upon all flesh; and your sons and daughters shall prophesy, your old men shall dream dreams, your young men shall see visions" (Joel 2:28). And continuing, Peter speaks directly of Christ's promise: "Therefore being by the right hand of God exalted, and having received of the Father the promise of the Holy Ghost, he has shed forth this which you now see and hear" (Acts 2:33). The Cluniac miniature not only depicts the Descent of the Holy Spirit but, following closely the text of Acts 2 and in particular Peter's explanation of the miracle, indicates that the Descent of the Spirit is doubly a fulfillment, first of the Old Testament prophecy and then of God's promise.[176] The artist has assigned to Peter, who was also the patron saint of Cluny, a central place as the one who first understood and explained the apostles' mission. The prominence of Christ and Peter in this scene gives vivid expression to the idea of the reforming papacy that Peter (and hence the pope) is the "vicarius Christi."[177]

lar Christ in the second Bible of St. Martial of Limoges, Paris, B.N. lat. 8, vol. 1, fol. 91 (*L'art roman à Saint-Martial de Limoges*, pl. 27). The extended arms of Christ in the Last Judgment at S. Angelo in Formis and at Berzé-la-Ville seem to be connected with this type, but are perhaps independent of the latter, since they may be understood through the specific content alone. But the gesture of Christ on the tympanum of Vézelay, though motivated by the subject, is more likely to have been influenced by a model like the miniature of the Cluny lectionary.

172. See A. Fabre, "L'iconographie de la Pentecôte," *Gazette des Beaux-Arts*, LXV, 1923, pp. 33-42. His view, in opposition to E. Mâle's reading of the scene as the Descent of the Holy Spirit, has been accepted by several scholars (cf. Mercier, *Les primitifs français*, pl. 99, E. Kitzinger, ART BULLETIN, XXXI, 1949, pp. 277, 278, n. 49) and is now canonized in Réau's *L'iconographie de l'art chrétien*, II, pp. 567ff., 592, where the versions in Vézelay and the Limoges sacramentary, as well as the Cluny miniature, are interpreted as the Mission of the Apostles or Christ's Promise and not the Pentecostal Descent of the Spirit. Seeliger, according to Réau, supports Mâle's view.

173. Reproduced in Fabre, *op.cit.*, p. 37. Cf. also the miniature in the Limoges sacramentary, cited in note 166.

174. Porter, *Romanesque Sculpture*, ill. 50, the tympanum of the North door of the narthex. It is mistakenly called an "Ascension" by Porter. The adjoining central tympanum at Vézelay could hardly have been intended then as an image of Christ's reappearance which was already represented on the side door. Christ's presence among the apostles in the scene of the Pentecost (leaving no place for Peter in the center below Him) fuses in a highly original way the outpouring of the Holy Spirit and the powerful transcendent Christ who is shown in a mandorla and among the clouds, His head rising through the break at the crown of the tympanum. In a North French manuscript of the 11th century, Paris, Arsenal MS 592, in a scene which is unquestionably Christ's Reappearance to the Apostles after the Resurrection (fol. 105), He floats above ground, a full standing figure with arms outstretched as on the cross, above and among the apostles; there are no rays. Below this scene is a painting of the next episode, the Doubting Thomas.

175. The text of Joel 2:28, quoted by Peter in Acts 2, was a reading in Cluny during Pentecost—see Albers, *Consuetudines Monasticae*, I, p. 77.

176. The "Ecce" prefixed to the promise in Christ's inscription, replacing the "Et" of Luke 24:49, indicates that it is the fulfillment, the Pentecostal outpouring of the Spirit itself.

177. See Michele Maccarrone, "Vicarius Christi, Storia del titolo papale," *Lateranum*, N.S. XVIII, Rome, 1952, pp. 94, 95, for the use of the expression "vicarius Christi" for the pope by Peter the Venerable, abbot of Cluny, and earlier by Peter Damian, the friend of abbot Hugo.

The frequent rendering of the Liberation of Peter from Prison ("Petrus in vinculis") in Cluny and its priories, as in the miniatures in Paris, B.N. lat. 1087 and N.A. lat. 2246, and on capitals at Vézelay and Moissac, may be connected with Cluniac supprot of the papacy, struggling with its secular opponents. In 1079 Pope Gregory sent to Alfonso VI, the

The Roman source of the Italo-Byzantine style in Cluny is confirmed by the character of another work of this trend in Cluny, the greatest of all: the frescoes of Berzé-la-Ville, a little priory near Cluny where the abbot Hugo often stayed and conducted affairs in the last years of his long life.[178]

The surviving paintings of the apse (Figs. 44-48) were done by an artist of great conviction who was able to realize with impressive force figures of spiritual authority that revive for us the ideal physiognomy of the Gregorian reform. Here the Italo-Byzantine style appears as a powerful means of expression, with a grandeur of rhythm and scale that ennobles the single figures and the whole composition. Details of ornament that in the Parma miniatures rival the figures in interest are marginal in the frescoes and of far less weight. The forms and ornament of the great surmounting dome and towers in the miniature (Colorplate II) reappear surprisingly at Berzé-la-Ville inverted on a vase at the spring of the arch soffit, from which issues a narrow band of foliage.[179] The conception of the painting of the apse-vault on a blue ground, with a clear gradation of figures from the giant central Christ to Peter and Paul and the apostles, to the lesser figures of Lawrence and Vincent, and finally to a pair of unknown bishop or abbot saints who are cut at the knees (Figs. 45-47), recalls the traditional mosaics of the Roman basilicas. In Berzé the hierarchically ordered whole has a more compact and dramatically focused aspect; the rhythm of arched lines and the contrasts of size are like the compositions of the great Romanesque sculptured tympana.

The series of busts of male and female martyrs below and the martyrdoms of Vincent (or Lawrence) and Blaise (Fig. 48) have been interpreted by Grabar as an additional sign of direct dependence on Roman art.[180] I do not doubt that the style has close connections with Rome—the similarities to the paintings in Santa Pudenziana seem to me sufficiently strong evidence—but the choice of saints is not a convincing proof. While listed in the Roman martyrology, these saints are also in the old Cluny calendar, and beside them are others like Denis and Quentin who are obviously French. Vincent was specially honored at Cluny and so was Blaise. Even the unusual Consortia and Florentia appear in the Cluny calendar and in a Cluny lectionary of the lives of saints.[181]

The relations of the Berzé painter to Italian art are a problem that calls for further study. It is hard to agree with the opinion expressed by Deschamps and Thibout that already formed

Spanish patron of Cluny, a golden key containing filings of Saint Peter's chains (Gregory, *Register*, VII, 6). But the same theme is also represented in a miniature of ca. 1000 from the Cathedral of Autun (Paris, Arsenal MS 1169) and on a Romanesque capital in that cathedral.

178. On his residence at Berzé see H. Diener, in *Neue Forschungen über Cluny und die Cluniacenser* von J. Wollasch, H.-E. Mager und H. Diener, hrsg. von G. Tellenbach, Freiburg, 1959, pp. 369, 371-373. The oldest document dates from 1093 (Bruel, *Recueil des chartes*, no. 3666). See Diener, pp. 414, 415, for a large list of monks and priors who were with Hugo at Berzé-la-Ville, as evidenced by their signatures on documents drawn up in Berzé during the last fifteen years of Hugo's life.

On the paintings, see Mercier, *Les primitifs français*, pp. 23-80, pls. 1-65; Koehler, *Dumbarton Oaks Inaugural Lectures, 1940*, pp. 61-87; Deschamps and Thibout, *La peinture murale*, pp. 89ff.; E. W. Anthony, *Romanesque Frescoes*, Princeton, 1951, pp. 135ff., figs. 271-276; A. Grabar, "Peintures murales, notes critiques," *Cahiers Archéologiques*, VI, 1952, pp. 185, 186; Grabar and Nordenfalk, *Romanesque Painting*, pp. 103-109, with colorplates.

179. Cf. the baptismal font in a painting at Sta. Pudenziana, Rome, for related forms (Ladner, *Jahrbuch der kunsthistorischen Sammlungen in Wien*, 1931, fig. 52; Anthony, *Romanesque Frescoes*, fig. 79).

180. *Romanesque Painting*, pp. 106ff.

181. The Cluniac calendar and litany in the 11th century can be reconstructed from various Cluniac manuscripts: Paris, B.N.N.A. lat. 2246, 2261, 2390 and lat. 13371, with lives of saints, and the *Consuetudines* of Bernard (B.N. lat. 13875) and Udalricus (N.A. lat. 638). For Denis and Quentin, see B.N.N.A. lat. 2246, fols. 153v, 166v; Dorotheus and Gorgonius appear in 13875 (fol. 180v, fol. 83–Sept. 9), Florentia in the litany in 13875, fol. 84, Consortia in N.A. lat. 2261, fol. 26v. In the *Consuetudines* of Udalricus, composed in the 1080's, is noted the feast: "In depositione Consortiae virginis" (Migne, *Pat. lat.*, CXLIX, col. 654); in the earlier Cluniac *Consuetudines "Farfenses"* (ca. 1040-1049), the feast days of Consortia and Florentia are singled out together in sequence (Albers, *Consuetudines Monasticae*, I, p. 81), and the Gospel readings for their feasts are of Matthew 25, the parables of the wise and foolish virgins and of the merchant, which pertain to the kingdom of heaven and the Last Judgment. Five of the six female saints at Berzé carry lamps. The choice of these saints, as of the lamps, need not depend then, as Grabar thinks, on Italian models. The painting of the wise virgins occurs, as he observes, already in the 9th century in Gorze, near Metz, later a focal point of the Cluniac reform.

I wish to thank Mrs. Jane Rosenthal for verifying the manuscript references for me.

French artists, accompanying Hugo on one of his trips to Italy, could by observing Italian painting have absorbed so much of the foreign style.[182] I have been unable to find in Berzé, at least in the figures of the apse vault, as pervading a trace of native Burgundian art as in the colophon miniatures. Apart from the ornament, which includes several motifs of the Parma Codex and which might be the work of an assistant,[183] the forms at Berzé that appear elsewhere in Burgundy are either Italian or Byzantine or so generally Western that one cannot infer from these alone the native region of the painter.[184] There is, however, something of the *élan* of the Romanesque sculptured portals of Burgundy in the free partitioning of the painted wall and in the artist's bold violation of the architectural form—he carries down the painted edge of the apse arch diagonally across the side wall instead of vertically along the piers.[185] Besides the eruptive effect of Christ's hands, feet and halo crossing the mandorla, which reminds us of the great Christ of Vézelay, there are the apostle's feet treading the ground line and the executioner's arm and sword breaking the edge of the frame. But this freedom in monumental design is a Western trait that can be found in Italian churches since the early Christian period and was still practiced there in the eleventh and twelfth centuries. A deeper study of French and Italian painting of the period about 1100 is needed before we can distinguish fully the Italian from the native Burgundian elements in the art of the master of Berzé-la-Ville.

Professor Grabar, who regards him as French, would place his work at least fifty years later than the accepted date.[186] The style, according to Grabar, is too advanced for 1100 but agrees with the Romanesque stage of Italo-Byzantine art in the second half of the twelfth century, and surely not before 1150.[187] His comparison of the frescoes with mosaics of the apses of San Clemente and Santa Maria in Trastevere in Rome and also with Sicilian mosaics dated after 1148 seems to me mistaken. I do not find their distinctive features in the frescoes, which look to me much closer to paintings of the earlier Roman school, like those of San Clemente, Sant'Elia at Nepi, and the oratory of Santa Pudenziana.[188] On the other hand, the similarity of intimate detail to the Cluniac manuscripts (the Parma Codex, the Cluny lectionary in Paris and the Montreal leaf) makes it clear that the frescoes are contemporary with these works which, because of the accompanying script and ornament, cannot be dated after the beginning of the twelfth century.

The relation of the painter of the Cluny lectionary to Roman art and his place within the Italianate

182. *La peinture murale*, pp. 89ff. Oursel, in *Bulletin annuel des Amis de Cluny*, IX, Cluny, 1955, pp. 1-8, thinks that the painter was an Italian. A more likely author of the Berzé fresco, I believe, is a Burgundian artist taught early in his career, if not from the start, by an Italian master.

183. The complex palmette and scroll ornament on the upper molding of the dado is like that of the borders of the Parma Codex, fol. 18v, 19, 72v.

184. E.g., the big rosettes on the band at the base of the apse vault and on the chasuble of the bishop saint at the lower right of Christ appear in 1650, fol. 102v (Gotiscalc) and in the Montreal miniature (Fig. 50). The acanthus rinceaux on the vault and the interlaced spirals are like the initial ornament of the Parma Codex. Note also the vase with rosette and acanthus ornament on the soffit at Berzé. The perspective meander of 1650 occurs there below the apse windows (Mercier, pl. XV), but this is a widespread motif in mural painting since the 9th century. Another element, found also in the Parma Codex, fol. 102v, is the forked foliate end of the spiral on the crozier of one of the abbots at Berzé, like Gotiscalc's crozier.

185. On this feature of Romanesque art, see my remarks in "Über den Schematismus in der romanischen Kunst," *Kritische Berichte*, 1932-33, pp. 1-21. In 2246, the angel of the Annunciation, the Christ of the Pentecost, the cross of the Crucifixion, and Saint Mark's scroll all break through their frames; cf. also the bull in the Montreal miniature.

186. *Cahiers Archéologiques*, 1952, pp. 185, 186. See also his *Romanesque Painting*, pp. 103-109, where he dates the Berzé murals "mid-12th century (?)" on p. 108. He argues that the style is based on the art of the Comnene dynasty, and that "it is difficult to believe that the influence of this style could have reached far-away France before the middle of the 12th century." But there is a letter of Peter of Cluny, written to John Comnenos, in which the abbot recalls to the Byzantine emperor that his father Alexis (1081-1118) gave many gifts ("precious ornaments") to places across the sea, including Cluny and its dependent abbey of La Charité-sur-Loire (*Pat. lat.*, CLXXXIX, cols. 260-262). Grabar's collaborator, C. Nordenfalk, *ibid.*, p. 190, places both the frescoes and N.A. lat. 2246 after the Parma manuscript, without proposing a more definite date. Oursel, *Bulletin annuel des Amis de Cluny*, IX, 1955, defends the early dating.

187. His view has been accepted by Garrison, *Studies*, II, p. 42, n. 3.

188. On Sta. Pudenziana, see Mercier, *Les primitifs français*, pls. XLVIII, XLIX (but the Italian works look provincial beside those at Berzé); cf. also the frescoes of S. Pietro, Toscanella (Tuscania), Garrison, *Studies*, III, fig. 239, p. 199, and Isermeyer, *Jahrbuch der Bibliothek Hertziana*, II, 1938, figs. 255, 256 (Peter cycle), 263 (Ascension), 268 (angel of apse); the frescoes of the old Lateran Palace chapel, Entombment of St. John the Evangelist (Garrison, II, 4, pp. 180ff., figs. 195-202); and Vatican lat. 12958, the Pantheon Bible, ca. 1100.

group in Cluny are difficult to state precisely. While sharing so many features with the frescoes, his forms have another accent and rhythm than those of the apse vault of Berzé-la-Ville, where the folds have become in places great whorls of arbitrary lines around an almond-shaped core. Are these differences purely individual variations of a common style? Or does the miniaturist proceed from another current in the common Roman art, perhaps from a specialized tradition of manuscript painting? In the Cluny lectionary, differences among the miniatures, too, suggest that all may not be by one hand; but if the Crucifixion looks weaker than the Pentecost and is possibly by another painter, it is still too close to Italian art to be attributed to a Burgundian assistant twice removed from the foreign source.

Unmistakably Italian in the pattern of the naked torso,[189] the conception of Christ on the cross (Fig. 38), with the feet descending below the ground line of the attending figures, is like that of Italian Romanesque crucifixes where Mary and John are placed together on one side of Christ as in the Cluny miniature.[190] This painting has several features in common with the Italianate pages of the Parma Codex, and even with those of the Ildefonsus master. The borders of gold, silver, and purple belong to the same artistic milieu; the division of the frame of the Crucifixion into little compartments with varying motifs occurs also in the Parma Codex,[191] and we find among these motifs the curious form that appears in the latter on the column in Fig. 1. In the posture of Christ, the arms and hands are distinctly Germanic; the gesture of the Virgin, too, comes from Northern art.[192] But these details might have appeared in an Italian style already saturated, like the initial ornament, with Northern types.

In the Montreal miniature (Fig. 50), which is probably the work of the lectionary painter, we discern many similarities to the colophon master. The evangelist holds his pen exactly like Gómez and the edge of the desk is scalloped as in the Parma page, though on the outside. His seat is of the same type as Gotiscalc's in shape and ornament. The scroll, curved and rising, repeats a form that is found in the Berzé fresco as well as in the Cluny lectionary,[193] but recalls also the floating or descending scrolls in Germanic portraits of the evangelists.[194] [195]

From these relationships it appears that the painter of the Parma colophon responds to more than one Italianate artist in Cluny. He is like the chief painter of the Cluny lectionary in some details of folds and like the Berzé master in others. He combines the *cloisonné* lighting of the first with the parallel lines along the contours in the fresco; but these lights are more broken and varied, even capricious in form. His figures are shorter and heavier and more rigidly symmetrical

189. For a detail of the torso, see Mercier, *Les primitifs français*, pl. 97.

190. Cf. E. B. Garrison, *Italian Romanesque Panel Painting*, Florence, 1949, pp. 183ff., nos. 456ff. and especially no. 459 (Sta. Chiara, Assisi, crucifix), and E. Sandberg-Vavalà, *La croce dipinta italiana*, Verona, 1929, figs. 15, 51, 55, 56, 58, 66, 67, 78, 79, 82, 92, 97, 101, 112, 407, etc.

The two angels above the cross are an Italian feature of Byzantine origin. They appear in the fresco of S. Urbano alla Caffarella, Rome (1011; Ladner, *Jahrbuch der kunsthistorischen Sammlungen in Wien*, figs. 75, 76) and on the Farfa ivory box (1071-1072, from Monte Cassino; Bloch, *Dumbarton Oaks Papers*, No. 3, 1946, fig. 250). Probably Italian, too, is the gabled form of the field of the miniature of the Dormition of the Virgin in the lectionary (fol. 122v; Mercier, *La peinture clunysienne*, pls. CIV-CVI). It is typical for Italian wood panels with the enthroned Virgin and Child. Such a panel is represented at Assisi in the Giottesque fresco of an episode at the funeral of Saint Francis. For preserved examples, mainly Tuscan and of the 13th century, see Garrison, *Italian Romanesque Panel Painting*, pp. 78ff.

191. On fols. 80ff. (figs. 24, 25x, y, 26h, i, l, x, y, 27w).

192. Cf. the Bavarian manuscript, Bamberg, Staatsbibl. Lit. 2; Bange, *Bayerische Malerschule*, fig. 65. The same Northern form of the arms and hands of Christ appears in the fragmentary fresco at Domène (Isère), a Cluniac priory dedicated in 1058; Deschamps and Thibout, *La peinture murale*, fig. 9, p. 49.

193. Cf. the scrolls of Peter and Paul in Berzé (Figs. 45, 46) and the bust of St. Mark in the lectionary, fol. 70v (Fig. 39). For a similar scroll, cf. the Moses on the tympanum of La Charité-sur-Loire (Porter, *Romanesque Sculpture*, ill. 115).

194. Cf. Mainz, Dombibliothek MS 974 (s.XI), Mark and Luke; St. Omer, the enamel and copper Mosan base of a cross (J. Braun, *Meisterwerke der deutschen Goldschmiedekunst*, Munich, 1922, I, pl. 51); and the Eilbertus altar in Vienna, *ibid.*, pl. 64.

195. The feet of the Montreal evangelist are curiously like those of a figure in a Trier manuscript, Paris, B.N. lat. 8851 (Goldschmidt, *German Illumination*, II, pl. 11). The scalloped arcature of the seat, which is like that in 2246 (and unlike the Parma Codex, where the arches of the footstool rest on distinct dwarf supports as in Byzantine art), is a favorite motif of the Master of the Registrum Gregorii (cf. Goldschmidt, *German Illumination*, II, pls. 7, 8, and our Fig. 68; and Nordenfalk, *Münchener Jahrbuch der bildenden Kunst*, I, 1950, figs. 9, 10, 13, 14).

than those of the other Italianate artists; and he elaborates the breaks in the folds beyond expressive and mimetic needs for their interest as a complex pattern, as he does with the lights.[196] The same T-shaped motif of white lines that we find in 2246 and Berzé along the brow and nose, with a light dot above the nose, is also applied by the colophon painter. In the Parma Codex, however, the dark dot between nose and mouth is more as in the Cluny lectionary than in Berzé, where this spot is attached in the Byzantine manner to the line of the nose.[197] The eye and brow in the latter are more fully arched and closed than in the corresponding form of both the lectionary and the colophon miniatures. In this expressive detail we may see, perhaps, an example of the basic difference of sentiment in the graver, more concentrating art of the Berzé master. These peculiarities in the use of Greek conventions make it probable that the colophon painter depends more on a miniaturist, who might have been the lectionary painter or his teacher, than on the author of the frescoes.

The reverse possibility, that the painter of the lectionary formed his style by purifying the art of the colophon master, seems to me unlikely.[198] (The script of the Parma Codex, we shall see later, is more advanced than that of the lectionary; but this argument is not conclusive for dating—since old and young scribes worked in the same scriptorium together.) If contemporary, I think it more likely that the colophon painter acquired the Byzantine forms from the painters of the lectionary and of Berzé-la-Ville (or their Italian teachers) and set them in a whole bedecked with native ornament and architectural detail.

Most interesting for the question of the links between the Parma Byzantinizing miniatures and Italian art is the fact that there were at Cluny around 1100 at least three, if not four, painters who worked in an Italo-Byzantine manner. Their differences and similarities are hard to evaluate for judging their relative age and distance from the parent Italian style. The master of the lectionary, we have seen, is not just a pupil of the Berzé mural painter; the Parma miniaturist is distinct from both, while agreeing with them in many elements of his art. Whether one attributes the Montreal leaf to the lectionary master or to another painter with the same tradition, it confirms the general unity of the school at Cluny by its close relation to both the frescoes and the colophon miniatures in different details.

For the presence of an Italian artist in Cluny there is an indirect literary indication. In the decade after Hugo's death a great Bible of remarkable beauty was made at Cluny by three men, Albert of Trier, Peter the Librarian, and Opizo.[199] The first of these must be the scribe, Albert the German, who was close to Hugo and accompanied him at Berzé where he signed a charter in 1107.[200] Opizo is an Italian name, and Peter may well be French.[201] The collaboration of these three is in the spirit of Cluniac art of the time, when Germanic, Italian and native forms were combined.

The library of Cluny possessed several manuscripts of this period that were imported from Italy and show an Italian variant of the Germanic initial ornament of the eleventh century.[202]

196. Cf. Gómez's right arm in the Parma Codex, fol. 102v, with Lawrence at the left in Berzé (Mercier, *Les primitifs français*, pl. 38; less clear in our Fig. 45) and Gómez on fol. 102, with the same Lawrence, with the Montreal figure and with an apostle at the left of the Pentecost in 2246 (Fig. 37). In general, the colophon painter, while working on a much smaller scale than the artist of Berzé, is more detailed and graphic; this is evident in the execution of the same motif: the Italian egg-and-dart, which is handled more broadly in Berzé (Mercier, *Les primitifs français*, pl. 23).

197. It is attached to the nose line at Sant'Angelo in Formis (Grabar, *Romanesque Painting*, pp. 35, 38), but is placed between nose and mouth in the frescoes of S. Pietro, Civate (*ibid.*, pp. 24, 27) and in some miniatures from Rome, as in the interesting homiliary, Vatican lat. 1267-1270.

198. This is the view of Carl Nordenfalk, *Romanesque Painting*, p. 190, who says that the style of the Parma painter (B) appears again "in a somewhat more developed form" in the miniatures of 2246 and the frescoes of Berzé.

199. See Marrier, *Bibliotheca Cluniacensis*, col. 1645.

200. See Bruel, *Recueil des chartes*, v, nos. 3862, 3869, 3873. He signs himself "Albertus Teutonicus."

201. The "Petrus Armarius" who helped Albert is probably the same scribe who wrote the charter published by Bruel. *Recueil des chartes*, v, no. 3798, dated 1100, and signed himself "Petrus Cluniacensis ecclesie armarius." It is not indicated in the colophon of the Bible, however, that any of the three men was a painter or illuminator.

202. Cf. Paris, B.N.N.A. lat. 1458, Jerome on Ezekiel (no. 193 of the mid-12th century catalogue of the Cluny

We may suppose that when Hugo undertook to build the new abbey church of Cluny in 1088, on a scale rivaling that of St. Peter's in Rome, he invited to Cluny several painters from Italy, where he had traveled in 1083 and had seen the new magnificence of Monte Cassino.[203] In this Campanian center, the birthplace of Benedictine monasticism, with which Hugo then established confraternity, he could admire not only works ordered from Constantinople by the abbot Desiderius, but also the products of immigrant Greeks who had helped to form a native group of monk-artists at the urging of the same abbot Desiderius. The rebuilding of Cluny, began in 1088 under Hugo, was perhaps inspired by the sight of the new church of Monte Cassino, consecrated in 1071.

There are, we have seen, significant similarities between the art of the colophon master and the manuscripts made under Desiderius. But the style of Berzé is not of the Cassinese type, and study of the lectionary and the Parma book convinces me that the likeness to Monte Cassino is too broad or incidental to justify the view that these works depend *directly* on the Campanian center. More plausible is the idea of a Roman source, which has already been discussed. It is supported by the detailed resemblance of the Byzantinizing art in Cluny to Roman frescoes and manuscripts and it is intelligible in the light of the close relations of Cluny with the papacy and her old and persistent interest in several abbeys and priories in Rome.[204]

If we assume that there were at Cluny around 1100 several artists painting in the Italo-Byzantine manner, whether Italians or taught by Italians, we can understand better not only the diversity of the works in Cluny, but also the varied character of those Italianate forms elsewhere in France and especially in Cluniac abbeys. I have referred before to related styles in Burgundy at Cîteaux after about 1110[205] and also at St.-Benigne in Dijon;[206] we find them in a number of manuscripts from Limoges of the late eleventh and early twelfth centuries,[207] at St.-Savin in the frescoes, and in manuscripts from Angers.[208]

In the Bible from St.-Martial of Limoges (Paris, Bibl. Nat. MS lat. 8) are striking parallels to Hand B of the Parma Codex, clearly the work of painters who had studied the style of an artist like the Colophon master (Figs. 52-54).[209] The first initial of the book (vol. I, fol. 1), it is interesting to note, is framed with panels of ornament that strongly suggest the borders of the Parma manuscript, designed by the Ildefonsus painter. The miniature of Jerome standing before Damasus in the preface to the Pentateuch (vol. I, fol. 4v; Fig. 52) recalls the page of Gómez and Gotiscalc in Parma. The painted calligraphic white lights on the leg of Gómez have become a complex drawing of hatched black lines of varied pattern—a clear example of the translation of the neo-Byzantine painting style into a Romanesque technique of drawing. In another miniature,

library, Delisle, *Fonds de Cluni*, p. 103); N.A. lat. 1439, Ambrose on Luke (no. 95 of the old catalogue, *ibid.*, pp. 45, 46). In N.A. lat. 1491, p. 268, the ornament of the initial I has a decidedly Italian appearance. Italian manuscripts of the late 11th and early 12th century appear also in the remains of the libraries of Cluniac houses, e.g., Moissac (Paris, Bibl. Nat. lat. 2213, Gregory on Job, and lat. 3862, Burchard's Canons) and St.-Martial of Limoges (lat. 2056, Augustine, City of God).

203. Hugo's visit to Monte Cassino in 1083 and the resulting confraternity of the two abbeys (recorded in the Chronicon Casinense, lib. III, Migne, *Pat. lat.*, CLXXIII, col. 790) are ignored by Prof. G. de Francovich who, in rejecting the supposed influence of Monte Cassino on Cluniac art—an influence that has been assumed by others on insufficient grounds—also denies any significant contact between the two abbeys under Hugo. See his article cited in note 146 above, pp. 507ff.

204. Perhaps painters called from Italy to Cluny by abbot Hugo painted the interior of the church in 1088-1100, while their native pupils produced the miniatures and the frescoes of Berzé-la-Ville. A possibility that I have not explored for lack of documents is the mediating role of the Cluniac dependencies in the North of Italy.

205. See Oursel, *La miniature du XIIe siècle*, cited in note 8 above.

206. Cf. Montpellier, Bibl. de la Faculté de Médecine, H 30, fol. 165; Nordenfalk (and Grabar), *Romanesque Painting*, p. 155 (colorplate).

207. Paris, B.N. lat. 8, 1987, 5296A.

208. Cf. Paris, B.N.N.A. lat. 1390, life of St. Aubin, ca. 1100, and Amiens, Bibl. mun. Fonds L'Escalopier MS 2, psalter of late 11th century; V. Leroquais, *Les Psautiers manuscrits latins des bibliothèques publiques de France*, Planches, pls. XXV, XXVI (pls. XXIII, XXIV of the same manuscript are in a more linear Romanesque style). I have noted a trace of the Italo-Byzantine in nearby Vendôme, Bibl. mun. MS 193, fol. 2v.

209. On lat. 8, see J. Porcher, in the *Catalogue de l'Exposition, L'Art Roman à Saint-Martial de Limoges, Les Manuscrits à Peintures*, no. 33, pp. 51-55, 66, 67, pls. XV-XVII, figs. 20-23. Porcher ignores the Italo-Byzantine factor here, but in the catalogue of the exhibition, *Byzance et la France Médiévale*, Bibliothèque Nationale, 1958, p. 64, no. 115, he writes: "Byzance y est présente, mais sans doute par l'entremise arabe d'Espagne"—a judgment that I do not understand.

in the preface to Joshua and Judges (vol. I, fol. 81), Jerome sits writing on a scroll held upward (Fig. 54), as in the Cluny lectionary, the Montreal leaf, and Berzé; here we see also the nested V folds and the long lines parallel to the contours of arm and sleeve—other devices of the Italo-Byzantine style. I have no doubt that in St.-Martial, which had been subject to Cluny since 1063, there were available before 1100 several works in the Italo-Byzantine manner of the mother house and that these works already showed the diversity of its practice at Cluny. In a Limoges manuscript of Saint Augustine on the Psalms (Paris, Bibl. Nat. lat. 1987; Fig. 58), which may be earlier than the Bible (lat. 8), the Italianate style is broader, more painterly and spontaneous, and suggests rather the hand of a fresco painter.

In a manuscript of the Life of Saint Martial (Paris, Bibl. Nat. lat. 5296A) we meet another offshoot of the Cluny style, heavily charged with ornament in the lighting of the drapery (Fig. 55).[210] A few features—the drawing of the brow hairs under the tonsure, the modeling of the head by white lines along the brows and wrinkles, the form of the brows and eyelids—are enough to betray the painter's source in a work of the Italo-Byzantine current.[211] That his models included a miniature like the painting of Gómez in the Parma Codex (fol. 102) appears not only in the details already mentioned, but in the accessory objects: the leafy growth at the base of the writing-table, the marbled columns, the caps and bases with curled leaves, the curtains, the bead ornament of the seat. Their connection with Cluny is confirmed by the modeling of arms and legs with the cloisonné forms and lighting. The Limoges painter has absorbed the foreign elements into a style which was essentially linear, flat, and minutely ornamented. The big gold bands of the costume—immense patches of brilliance—repress the convex forms beneath and make an independent restless pattern that is unsculptural and inorganic and is seen with the bands in the architecture overhead. On a smaller scale, the flicker of the little units of masonry, tiles, windows, and arches, is taken up in the lights on the costume and the curtains, and on the seat and columns. What remains large and sculptural amid the ornamental detail in the Cluny miniature has disappeared in the Limoges painting, where the dense hatchings of white on the draped body have little if any sense as modeling.[212]

In all these French works the Italian forms have become more schematic, linear and ornamental than at Cluny, but in some instances looser and more impulsive in brushwork. In Italy, too, the Byzantinizing style shows a great range of qualities, with more or less schematic forms and reductive features.[213] But for none of the other French works would one raise the question, as for Berzé and the Cluny lectionary, of a possible Italian authorship; their French Romanesque character is evident in numerous details that connect them with the native tradition. They suggest, however, that if Cluny was the original point of diffusion in France, there must have been two, if not more, variants of the Italian style available at Cluny around 1100. At Stavelot also, where the Byzantine forms in the Bible of 1093-1097 are probably independent of Cluny, at least two types of Byzantine style are reflected in the miniatures.[214]

Before I conclude this study of the Byzantine factor in Cluniac painting, I must call attention

210. Garrison, *Studies*, II, pp. 42, 43, connects it with Monte Cassino, and places it in the early 12th century.

In the catalogue of the exhibition of Limoges, p. 66 (see note 209), Porcher says that this may be the volume written under the direction of Adémar de Chabannes, a monk of Limoges who lived ca. 988-1034. The script, the ornament and the painting are clearly no earlier than the end of the 11th century.

211. See Garrison, *Studies*, II, fig. 172 and p. 163, for a comparison with the much later Casanatense Bible, cod. 721 (his figs. 170, 171). The initial ornament of lat. 5296A includes blossoms with "sprung" and curled petals of Byzantine type. Similar foliate ornament appears in another Limoges manuscript, B.N. lat. 743, a breviary—beside initials of the Cluniac Ottonian style.

212. In other Limoges miniatures—e.g., in lat. 8—the hatched white lines emerge from a solid white highlight, a device that appears also in the paintings at Berzé-la-Ville.

213. An example is Florence, Bibl. Laurenziana, Pluteo 17, 27, fol. 6v (Matthew writing), a Roman evangeliary of the early 12th century–Garrison, *Studies*, II, p. 38, fig. 22–which may be compared with the Angers manuscript, B.N.N.A. lat. 1390.

214. See H. Swarzenski, *Monuments of Romanesque Art*, Chicago, 1955, figs. 224, 225, 251, 252, 356.

to its presence also in the work of the Ildefonsus master. What is Byzantine in his art, however, comes only in small part from the Italian current; certain elements have been transmitted through older Western tradition, and even through Ottonian art.

The small miniatures of the prophets inserted in the text (Figs. 18, 19, 29) recall in their place and format the Byzantine practice of representing busts of prophets and saints, often in isolated medallions, within the text or on the margins close to the passages that refer to them.[215] I do not know of so extensive a use of such bust portraits in the text of Western manuscripts before this time. The conversion of the circular medallion to a square or more complex rectilinear frame is in the spirit of Romanesque art, with its taste for fractioned and composite forms and its openness to the accidental in designing frames.[216] Similar portraits had appeared outside the text in Ottonian manuscripts, where effigies of rulers and personifications, formerly enclosed in medallions, were set in squares at the corners or cardinal points of a frontispiece frame.[217] In a Bavarian manuscript of the eleventh century the busts of the twelve apostles in rectangular frames are aligned in two vertical rows beside a central figure of Christ, a conception that was probably derived from a Byzantine plaque with superposed busts of the apostles in medallions or divided oblong strips.[218]

The parallel thin white lines on the parts of the costume bounded by dark folds seem to be of Byzantine origin (Figs. 3-7). Are they a sign that the newly imported Italian style at Cluny was already affecting the older native Romanesque? These serried lines are not designed for modeling as in the Byzantine practice. In most figures they are barely luminous; yet in spite of their decorative surface character they suggest the contemporary Italo-Byzantine method. One should not forget, however, that before this time Carolingian and Ottonian art showed a similar streaking of lines of light, sometimes in gold, inspired by older Byzantine art.[219] In Hand A's work it is not applied alike to all figures. In the Christ in Glory (Fig. 21) we see a broader patching of light with an effect of true modeling; and on other pages (e.g. on the secular figures in Fig. 14) are long parallel streakings of light, sometimes comb-shaped, which are more pronounced than the short thin lines of white on the monks' costumes and resemble the streaks of light on certain figures in the Menologion of Basil II.[220] This variety is typical for the late eleventh century in the West, when a heritage of different styles from the preceding development, from late antiquity onward, provided a repertoire of types and elements for the artist's choice. In the Parma Codex the parallel lines of light, both the minute and the larger kind, may be a newly acquired feature, for they are absent in the first four miniatures and appear regularly in those that follow, though with unequal delicacy—perhaps introduced by the artist from a German model in the course of work, and after observation of the paintings of a fellow artist of the Italo-Byzantine trend.

215. Cf. Milan, Bibl. Ambrosiana, Cod. E.49-50 inf., homilies of Gregory Nazianzus (K. Weitzmann, *Illustrations in Roll and Codex*, Princeton, 1947, fig. 105); cf. also Paris, B.N. gr. 923, the Sacra Parallela of John of Damascus.

216. Note in 2246, fol. 70v (Fig. 39) a bust of St. Mark in a square which is broken by the halo and the scroll; at the base the frame is dented to make way for the capital V below. A question: is the cutting of the figures at the thighs and knees in 1650 (Figs. 11, 18, 19) connected with the similar cutting of the smaller figures in the apse painting at Berzé-la-Ville (Figs. 45-47)? Such a treatment appears later in Italian Romanesque tympana and in German art.

217. Cf. Paris, B.N. lat. 10501, sacramentary of Trier (later in Metz), Goldschmidt, *German Illumination*, II, pl. 15; lat. 8851, *ibid.*, pl. 16; Manchester, John Rylands Library, MS 98, *ibid.*, pl. 16, all from the school of Trier.

218. Munich, Staatsbibl. lat. 9476, a gospel book from Niederaltaich (Bange, *Bayerische Malerschule*, fig. 20). Bange, p. 30, cites other examples in Darmstadt MS 1946, a missal of the Echternach school, and a Reichenau carving in Paris.

219. Cf. the manuscripts of the Carolingian Court school ("Ada") in Goldschmidt, *German Illumination*, I, pls. 37, 40, 43, II, pl. 18A; the fresco of the Descent into Limbo in S. Clemente, Rome, Anthony, *Romanesque Frescoes*, fig. 51; Reichenau manuscripts, Goldschmidt, *op.cit.*, II, pl. 6 (Codex Egberti), pl. 18B (Gero Codex), II, pl. 32 (Vatican, Barberini lat. 711), and the Pericope Book of Henry II, Munich lat. 4452, Grabar and Nordenfalk, *Early Medieval Painting*, p. 204 (colorplate); from France: Pierpont Morgan Library MS 641, from Mont St. Michel, H. Swarzenski, *Monuments of Romanesque Art*, fig. 174, and Paris, B.N. lat. 9436, sacramentary of St. Denis, V. Leroquais, *Les sacramentaires et les missels*, Paris, 1924, pls. 31, 32. Very close to the Parma miniatures are the thin white lines of light in the Vyšerad Coronation gospels of ca. 1085, a work of the Bohemian school strongly influenced by Bavarian art, H. Swarzenski and J. Květ, *Czechoslovakia, Romanesque and Gothic Illuminated Manuscripts*, Unesco, New York, 1959, pl. IV; cf. also the St. Vitus gospels in Prague Cathedral, *ibid.*, pl. X.

220. See *Il Menologio di Basilio II*, pls. 5, 9, 43, etc.

In that same miniature of Christ in glory another feature of East Christian origin, which undoubtedly came to Cluny from the pre-Romanesque art of Northern Europe, is the iconographic conception: the mandorla, with two arcs symbolizing heaven and earth as seat and footstool, and Christ with the blessing hand at his breast and the other hand holding the closed book on the upper edge. This posture gives compactness to the figure and accords with the outlook of this sober monastic artist; just as the other medieval type of Christ, with extended hand blessing and commanding, often attracts artists who display in their work a more impulsive, outgoing nature. All these elements of the image of Christ in glory, which are known in early Christian and Byzantine art,[221] had reached the West by the ninth century and were transmitted repeatedly in the successive vogues of the Byzantine during the Middle Ages, appearing often as thoroughly assimilated types with little if any trace of Byzantine style in the rendering.[222] They are especially common in Germany in the eleventh and twelfth centuries.[223]

A little detail in the Cluny miniature suggests dependence on a German source at some point in the line of descent: the dots that fill the background in the mandorla—a familiar feature in German wallpainting during this period.[224] Yet this element appears also in the mandorla of Christ at Berzé-la-Ville. In the Parma Codex the dots have lost the old Byzantine star pattern which is still visible in Berzé.[225]

221. For the mandorla with arc see Walter Cook, "The Earliest Painted Panels of Catalonia," ART BULLETIN, VI, 2, 1923, pp. 16ff.; cf. the ampullae of Monza and Bobbio (A. Grabar, *Les ampoules de terre sainte*, Paris, 1958, pls. VII, XXXIII); the mosaics of Hosios David and Hagia Sophia, Salonica (R. Berger, *Die Darstellung des thronenden Christus in der romanischen Kunst*, Reutlingen, 1926, fig. 57); the Zoë mosaic in Hagia Sophia, Istanbul (1028-1043; Rice, *Art of Byzantium*, pl. 133 and colorplate XIII); the mosaic of the Ascension, central dome, S. Marco, Venice; the mosaic of the Last Judgment, Torcello (Berger, *op.cit.*, fig. 115).

For the type of Christ, cf. the Last Judgment in Vatican gr. 699, Cosmas Indicopleustes (Berger, *op.cit.*, fig. 59); a relief in S. Marco, Venice (*ibid.*, fig. 50); the mosaic in Torcello (*ibid.*, fig. 46).

222. For the mandorla with arc in Western art, cf. London, Brit. Museum, Stowe MS 944, Liber Vitae, Winchester, 1016-1020 (E. G. Millar, *English Illuminated Manuscripts Xth-XIIIth Century*, Paris, Brussels, 1926, pl. 25a); Brit. Museum, Harley MS 2928, fol. 14v, from Solignac, s. XII in.; ivory carving, Rouen, s. XI (Berger, *Die Darstellung des thronenden Christus*, fig. 31); Dijon, Bibl. mun. MS 132, Jerome on Daniel (Oursel, *La miniature du XIIe siècle*, pl. XLV); Limoges enamel plaque, Christ in Majesty, Paris, Musée de Cluny; Tournus, crypt, fresco (Mercier, *Les primitifs français*, pls. LXXI, LXXIII); Rome, S. Clemente, fresco of the Ascension (847-853); Monte Cassino, codex 175M (915-934), Rule of St. Benedict (Ladner, *Jahrbuch der kunsthistorischen Sammlungen in Wien*, 1931, fig. 62); Tuscan sacramentary, New York, Pierpont Morgan Library MS 737, fol. 86 (E. B. Garrison, *Studies*, I, 1954, p. 178, fig. 279); Calci missal (*ibid.*, fig. 276); Parma, Baptistery portal (Berger, *op.cit.*, fig. 22); Burgo de Osma, Beatus on the Apocalypse, 1086 (J. Dominguez Bordona, *Códices Miniados Españoles, Catálogo*, Madrid, 1929, pl. 23–an influence from the North, probably from France).

For the type of Christ which goes back to a late classical secular image like the figure of Probianus on the Berlin diptych from Werden (H. Schnitzler, *Rheinische Schatzkammer*, figs. 160, 161), cf. Rome, S. Maria Antiqua, fresco (Grabar and Nordenfalk, *Early Medieval Painting*, p. 48); the Carolingian Gospels of St.-Médard de Soissons, Paris, B.N. lat. 8850, initial Q (Berger, *op.cit.*, fig. 36); a Carolingian ivory carving in Berlin (*ibid.*, fig. 27); the gold cover of the Codex Aureus, Munich lat. 14000, ca. 870 (H. Swarzenski, *Monuments of Romanesque Art*, fig. 20); fresco of 959, Sta. Maria delle Fratte, near Carpignano, S. Italy (N. H. Westlake, *History of Design in Mural Painting*, London, Oxford, II, 1905, p. 63, pl. LXXIV); Charlieu, tympanum, West door (Berger, *op.cit.*, fig. 73, Porter, *Romanesque Sculpture*, ill. 4); Dijon, Bibl. mun. MS 132 (Oursel, *La miniature du XIIe siècle*, pl. XLV); Tuscan sacramentary, Pierpont Morgan Library, MS 737 (Garrison, *loc.cit.*); Calci missal (*ibid.*).

Note that both features—the mandorla with the arc and the Christ with blessing hand at the breast—occur together in Morgan MS 737, the Calci missal, the Cîteaux manuscript, Dijon 132, and the Limoges enamel plaque in the Musée de Cluny, Paris.

223. For the mandorla, cf. Munich lat. 4456, Sacramentary of Henry II (Goldschmidt, *German Illumination*, II, pl. 72); Madrid, Codex Aureus from Speyer (made for Henry III at Echternach, 1043-46; *ibid.*, II, pl. 57); the Bamberg Apocalypse, fol. 10v; Vienna MS 791 (Swarzenski, *Salzburger Malerei*, fig. 71–from Mondsee); Bamberg, MS Lit. 2, from Freising (Bange, *Bayerische Malerschule*, fig. 63); and many other works reproduced by Berger, *Die Darstellung des thronenden Christus*, figs. 67 (Knechtsteden, fresco), 86 (Alpirsbach, tympanum), 108 (Freckenhorst, baptismal font), 109 (Burgfelden, fresco), 116 (Reichenau-Oberzell, fresco), etc.

For the Christ type, cf. the Madrid Codex Aureus from Echternach (see above); Vienna MS 791 (see above); the early stone relief at St. Emmeram, Regensburg (Berger, *op.cit.*, fig. 1); fresco at Schwarzrheindorf (*ibid.*, fig. 11).

Note that both features appear together in the Echternach Codex Aureus of Henry III, in Vienna 791, and on an ivory book-cover in Braunschweig (*ibid.*, fig. 33).

224. Cf. the frescoes at St. George, Oberzell-Reichenau (Berger, *op.cit.*, fig. 116), Burgfelden (*ibid.*, fig. 109), Knechtsteden (Clemen, *Die romanische Monumentalmalerei in den Rheinlanden*, fig. 187), Tournus, crypt (Mercier, *Les primitifs français*, pls. LXXI, LXXIII).

225. For the traces of stars on a blue ground, originally filled with glass or metal, in the Berzé mandorla, see Clemen, *Die romanische Monumentalmalerei*, p. 650, n. 16 (referring to the original publication by Lex and Martin in 1895). For stars in the mandorla, cf. the mosaic of the Ascension at S. Marco in Venice, the Bobbio ampulla (Grabar, *Les ampoules de terre sainte*, pl. XXXIII), a miniature from Reichenau in the New York Public Library (a gospel manu-

On the same page the conception of the four symbols, with heads turned back to gaze at Christ, is a French Carolingian invention that synthesizes older Eastern and Western types.[226] In Byzantine as in early East Christian art the four beasts are centrifugal, moving outward from the mandorla, like the horses of the Sun in classic imagery; while in Italy another early Christian type, with the four beasts turned in profile to Christ as if in adoration, is maintained throughout the Middle Ages—the exceptions are borrowings from Northern art.[227] In Parma the awkward repetition (instead of the expected symmetry) of the postures of lion and bull is adapted to the presence of the saint in prayer at the lower left. Yet we find this odd form on an old drawing of the tympanum of Cluny.[228] The deviation also had a precedent in the repeated parallel postures of the two beasts (as distinguished from a true symmetry) on canon tables in gospel manuscripts of the eleventh century in Bavaria.[229]

The placing of Ildefonsus in prayer below Christ in glory is typically Western, although combined with Byzantine features in the figure of Christ. In the West, since the ninth century, and often in the tenth and eleventh, even humble monastic figures were brought into the field below the heavenly Christ. In a miniature of the St. Gall school in Einsiedeln, ca. 900, the scribe kneels in prayer beneath an enthroned Christ.[230] Contemporary with the Parma Codex, a Benedictine monk is drawn in prayer before Christ in majesty in the Volturno chronicle, a work that like the Parma manuscript has both Northern and Italo-Byzantine forms.[231]

In the page from Cluny the Byzantine, Carolingian, and Ottonian elements have been fused into a distinctly Romanesque and even Burgundian whole, to judge by its similarity to the other works of the region. There is in the figure of Christ an aspect of the constructed and monumental, an accentuation of the axes of the body in contrast to the curves and angles of the surrounding forms, that is akin to the new stone sculpture of Burgundy, which has, however, a more expansive line. The older tympanum at Charlieu, from the period before 1100, offers a parallel in the conception of Christ.[232]

script of the 10th century), the tympana of Moissac and Conques, etc. The figure of Christ had already been painted on a starry ground in the 9th century on a vault of St. Faron at Meaux (Deschamps and Thibout, *La peinture murale*, p. 16).

226. On the types of the four symbols, see my article: "Two Romanesque Drawings in Auxerre and Some Iconographic Problems," *Studies in Art and Literature for Belle Da Costa Greene*, Princeton, 1954, pp. 338, n. 36, and p. 344.

227. Where they face Christ in Byzantine art, as in Parma, Pal. MS 5, fol. 5—a Greek gospel manuscript of the 11th or 12th century—one may infer a Western and probably an Italian influence. The symbols carry books and in the same miniature the four evangelists are shown writing, with Peter and Paul and two figures of the Old Testament.

228. See R. Berger, *Die Darstellung des thronenden Christus*, fig. 72 (lithograph by Sagot). In Professor Conant's restoration of the tympanum (see Joan Evans, *Cluniac Art of the Romanesque Period*, Cambridge, 1950, fig. 20, and K. J. Conant, "Mediaeval Academy Excavations at Cluny," *Speculum*, XXIX, 1954, p. 41, pl. XVc), the beasts are shown facing each other, on the uncertain authority of a poor engraving dated by Conant (*Speculum*, III, 1928, pp. 401ff., fig. 1) before 1810, when the church was demolished. The form in Sagot's lithograph of the tympanum appears also in his version of the painting in the apse of Cluny, where man and eagle face each other, the bull turns away from Christ and the lion turns his head back to see Christ (the whole reversed in the print). Sagot patterned his drawing perhaps on the central tympanum of Chartres. See Mercier, *Les primitifs français*, pl. LXVII.

229. Bange, *Bayerische Malerschule*, pls. 2, 21, 28, 39, 49, 52.

230. Einsiedeln, Stiftsbibl. cod. 17 (Merton, *Die Buchmalerei in St. Gallen*, pl. 33, no. 1; Prochno, *Das Schreiber- und Dedikationsbild*, pl. 19). Cf. the posture of Ildefonsus with the kneeling king in the Munich Prayer Book of Charles the Bald, Prochno, *op.cit.*, pl. 3 and the following examples. There is a close resemblance to the kneeling king at the feet of Christ in Majesty in the Echternach Codex Aureus from Speyer in Madrid, written for Henry III (1043-1046), Goldschmidt, *German Illumination*, II, pls. 57, 58. The Christ figure is related to the Christ in our miniature. For the king kneeling at the feet of Christ in a mandorla, see also the miniatures in the prayer book of the young Otto III (made for archbishop Willegis of Mainz, 975-1011) in the library of the Counts Schönborn in Pommersfelden, cod. 2940, reproduced in Grabar and Nordenfalk, *Early Medieval Painting*, pp. 209-210.

231. Vatican, Barberini lat. 2724, fol. 9v; Christ sits on the arc in a mandorla.

232. Porter, *Romanesque Sculpture*, 1923, ill. 4; R. Berger, *Die Darstellung des thronenden Christus*, fig. 73.

CHAPTER XII

THE PARMA CODEX AND BURGUNDIAN ART

What is native in the two styles of the manuscript? How are they related to the contemporary Burgundian art?

I shall not try to characterize the art of Burgundy in general. It has several different currents as well as stages, and we must admit that we know too little of the regional art of the tenth and eleventh centuries to be able to say what is native. The effort to place the styles of the Parma Codex more precisely within the varied whole of Burgundian art would pose new problems and take us beyond the limits of this study. But I shall consider here several relationships that illuminate certain features of our manuscript and of Cluniac art as a whole.

To neither the Ildefonsus nor the Colophon master can we apply the familiar characterizations of Burgundian art built on such highly individual works as the capitals of Cluny, the great tympana of Vézelay and Autun, or the initials of the Bible of Stephen Harding from Cîteaux. Whatever stylistic principles and details of form are shared by these works and the miniatures of the Parma Codex, the latter lack the intensity of feeling and the awakening to nature that animate the most original Burgundian art of this time. We are not surprised that in the manuscripts of Cluny the paintings are accompanied by initials with an older spiral foliate ornament, while artists elsewhere, even in Cluniac abbeys, overwhelm the initials with an exuberant imagery of the bestial, the demonic and grotesque, amazing in its spontaneous violence of movement. The spirited drawing of the early Cistercians, their dramatic rendering of action, their wit and drôlerie, are inconceivable in the ceremonious art of the two Cluniac painters. In expression these correspond rather to Cluny's conservative outlook, although their forms include advanced features of drawing, modeling and composition. The first hand borrows from a phase of German Imperial art, but its stable regular construction makes us think that qualities of more recent French art are latent in the France of 1100, at least in the disciplined conventual world of Cluny. The other hand, assimilating the Byzantine forms diffused from Monte Cassino and Rome, responds to Cluny's Italian ties, while adopting also details of form that come from the German sphere. Empire and papacy, as the twin supports of Cluniac ideals, engaged Cluny in a policy of reconciliation when these prime powers of Western Christendom conflicted.[233] In their somewhat impersonal acceptance of the foreign German and Italian forms, both artists were faithful to Cluny, the institution.

But this account of the matter is hardly complete, for in Berzé-la-Ville and the Paris lectionary the Italianate style has a greater purity and expressive force. And the capitals of the choir of Cluny, as works of architectural relief, belong to another sphere of artistic development than do the manuscripts and wall paintings and pose altogether new problems of form. Monumental sculpture, the most powerfully creative art of that time, was a field unknown or undeveloped in the preceding German and Italian schools. Figure carving in stone was not only a revived classic technique which the lay sculptors emulated after study of the abundant remains from the Gallo-Roman past; it called for a larger scale of artistic conception suited to the rapidly advancing architecture, and in turn endowed this architecture with a new face, in accord with the increased plasticity and expressiveness of the building mass—a speaking face that was addressed to the outer world and that affirmed through a legible imagery the presence of the spiritual church as a guiding integrating force.

233. This is clearly stated by Raynaldus, abbot of Vézelay and later archbishop of Lyons, in his Vita Hugonis, Migne, *Pat. lat.*, CLIX, cols. 903, 904, in speaking of Hugo's role in the conflict between Henry IV and Pope Gregory VII.

The programs of stone sculpture on portals, cloisters, and the interior of the church had an immensely stimulating effect on art. Compared to older sculpture in precious metals and ivory, stone carving was virile and secular, of greater impact, and imbued with something of the inventive spirit and daring of the new arts of building; its practitioners, who were most often lay artisans, open to nature and common life, brought into their work more of everyday experience.

In Burgundy there existed in the eleventh century—outside Cluny, and in Cluny, too—styles of drawing on which the sculptors and painters of the next generations could found their more intensely gestural art. In the manuscripts from St.-Bénigne of Dijon, of the mid-eleventh century, are figures with elaborately spun folds and angular bodies (Fig. 62) that anticipate the web of lines in the great Romanesque tympana.[234] A lectionary of the first half of the century from Cluny preserves a drawing of the martyrdoms of Peter and Paul, with the flying folds and the rich zigzag of pleated hems that were so favored in the twelfth century (Fig. 63).[235] We may suppose that similar styles also governed some of the mural paintings of that time. The beautiful capitals from the choir of Cluny seem to lie outside this tradition of complex line; they are built upon a sparser, more static type of post-Carolingian art which the sculptor infused with a new naturalness and grace in transposing the forms to high relief. Yet certain characteristic forms of the capitals, like the concentric folds of the thighs and legs, may be found not only on the great tympana of Vézelay and throughout the sculpture of the Burgundian region, but also in those rigid figures of the Ildefonsus master that we have compared with German art. Perhaps if we knew more of the art of Cluny during the eleventh century than what has survived in a few manuscripts of minor quality, the works of the period around 1100 would seem to us less isolated and uncoherent as a group. That there was at Cluny an art of monumental sculpture and painting earlier in the eleventh century can be inferred perhaps from the old accounts of the destroyed cloister and church of Odilo.[236] A drawing of a crowned Christ on the margin of a page in Paris (Bibl. Nat. MS Nouv. Acq. lat. 1455, fol. 112v) may be a copy of a mural painting of the eleventh century (Fig. 69); its tall figure and air of energy, its strong lines, which have also a suggestion of the Byzantine, set it apart from all that we learn about art in Cluny from the surviving miniatures and sculptures.[237]

I have implied that several characteristics of the first style of the Parma Codex can be found

234. Cf. Paris, B.N. lat. 11624 and 9518; the latter is dated 1031-1046, since it was given by the abbot Halinardus. See my article: "A Relief in Rodez and the Beginnings of Romanesque Sculpture in Southern France," *Studies in Western Art, Acts of the Twentieth International Congress of the History of Art* (September 1961, New York), Princeton, 1963, pp. 40-63. Cf. also Montpellier, Bibl. de la Faculté de Médecine, MS 76, fol. 81 (Ambrose), for a drawing of the Trinity and four angels, with traces of Byzantine forms, probably of Burgundian origin.

235. Paris, B.N.N.A. lat. 2390, fol. 32. It suggests a connection with the art of St. Gall; see Merton, *Die Buchmalerei in St. Gallen*, pls. 55-58, and Goldschmidt, *German Illumination*, I, pl. 72. Mlle. M. Th. D'Alverny informs me that the marginal notes in this manuscript were utilized by the scribes of the later lectionary of Cluny, B.N.N.A. lat. 2246.

236. See Jotsaldus, Vita Odilonis, Migne, *Pat. lat.*, 142, col. 908. Cf. also the reference to works of art in Odilo's church in the Consuetudines Farfenses of Cluny–B. Albers, *Consuetudines Monasticae*, I, pp. 9, 23-25 (a painted panel of the Virgin and Christ), 44, 54 ("eglyphinatum ex picturis variis"), 72, 82, 86, 183, 184; and the titulus of a painting transcribed by a hand of the 11th century on the last page of B.N.N.A. lat. 332, fol. 131v–"versiculi in capella sanctae resurrectionis" (Delisle, *Fonds de Cluni*, p. 90).

237. It is on the margin of John Chrysostom's homily (II) on Paul. The continuity of the cross in the halo with the outlines of the crown suggests that the artist was copying a model in which both objects were in gold.

Although such details of the beard as the spiral and circular lines resemble the forms in B.N.N.A. lat. 2246–cf. the apostles of the Pentecost and the Saint Mark (Figs. 37, 39)—the drawing, with its rapid cursive line, depends for its Byzantine aspect on another and earlier model than the Italo-Byzantine style that underlies B.N.N.A. lat. 2246; note, for example, the clavus on the right shoulder and breast and the meander of the edge of the tunic at the neck.

It was probably done in the middle or just after the middle of the 11th century, at the same time as the text. In several features it resembles the drawing of the Martyrdoms of Peter and Paul in Paris B.N.N.A. lat. 2390 (Fig. 63), which is of the first half of the century. The eyes, the drawing of the hand, the square crown, even the conception of Christ holding a scepter in one hand and what I take to be a cross in the other, may be matched in the figures of the earlier miniature.

Delisle, *Fonds de Cluni*, p. 101, calls the figure "Saint John," perhaps because of the "s" and the abbreviation mark over it, next to the halo (for "Iohannes"); but the interpretation seems to me mistaken. For a related conception compare the drawing of God the Father with crown and cross nimbus, holding a long cross-staff, in an Anglo-Saxon manuscript, the Pontifical of Sherborne (ca. 992-995), Paris B.N. lat. 943, fol. 5v; F. Wormald, *English Drawings of the Tenth and Eleventh Centuries*, London, 1952, fig. 4a.

in Burgundian art of the early twelfth century. The setting of the figures in a milieu—the use of a specific background that suggests a "surrounding" space—appears at the same time in the narrative scenes of the Bible of Stephen Harding,[238] and not long after in the capitals of Vézelay, Autun and Saulieu.[239] This background is often an architecture of columns and arches, but may also be a "landscape," a vegetation that fills the entire ground. In the capitals of Cluny, the single figures are placed inside a deep mandorla embedded in a richly modeled and curled foliage. The figures sometimes stand on a pedestal of arches (Vézelay, Autun) as on fol. 4v (Colorplate 1);[240] sometimes they are suspended above a ground line without touching it.[241] Although much in their work recalls previous sculpture in ivory and metal, the Romanesque stonecarvers are not simply reproducing old models, but searching and inventing; where they repeat the inherited forms, they build upon them freshly.

Also in some peculiarities of the figures the Burgundian artists share several traits with the painters of the Parma Codex. I have mentioned earlier the banding of the limbs with concentric lines so familiar in the sculpture and drawing of this time. The eye, drawn with a horizontal upper lid and curved lower one, is typical in the Cistercian manuscripts.[242] But this form, which is approached in Echternach, is common in France and England in the eleventh century. In Burgundian art, as in our manuscript, the three-quarters position of the head is the required form, although in Cîteaux the profile accompanies it and enlivens the contrast of individuals in action.[243] More striking is the intensity of gesture in Burgundian art, of which the scene of Jacob and his Sons in Parma (Fig. 15) has given us the most developed model among the Cluniac works. This lively gesticulation heightens the expressiveness of the tympana of Autun and Vézelay, especially in the enframing scenes of the mission of the Apostles. Characteristic is the paradoxical gesture of crossing the arms and hands which extend outside the body (Figs. 6, 11, 12, 20); we find it in the Stephen Harding Bible in the scenes of Haman and of Judith;[244] it is the gesture of the angel of the Annunciation on the early altar of Avenas.[245] While frequent in Burgundy, it is not exclusively of this region, but is a widespread Romanesque form, found also in Echternach miniatures of the eleventh century.[246]

Another interesting posture, the hand supporting the arm (Fig. 2), is given to Joseph on a relief in Charlieu.[247] The bent knees, the zigzag of the whole body, which we see several times in the Ildefonsus manuscript, is a common type in Burgundian sculpture, appearing in Vézelay, Autun and Montceaux-l'Étoile.[248] Still another peculiarity of the Parma Codex, the modeling of the legs by drawing the inner curve of the calf, reappears as a convention in a manuscript of Cîteaux.[249]

Romanesque, too, is the conception of the figure with opposed directions of the head and body (Fig. 20), a form that resembles a vital type in Greek art of the archaic period, when the painters

238. Cf. Oursel, *La miniature du XIIe siècle*, pls. 10, 12, and also the Psalter of Robert (Dijon MS 30), *ibid.*, pl. 1.

239. Porter, *Romanesque Sculpture*, II, ills. 30-37, 39, 46 (Vézelay), 70 (Autun), 53, 54, 56 (Saulieu), 107 (Fleury-la-Montagne). Cf. also Parma 1650, fol. 40v, Micah (Fig. 17), with the capital from Moûtier-St.-Jean at the Fogg Museum (*ibid.*, ill. 64).

240. Porter, *Romanesque Sculpture*, ills. 36, 37 (Vézelay), 79 (Autun), 88 (St. Paul-de-Varax). See note 72 above for the German examples.

241. Porter, *Romanesque Sculpture*, ill. 37 (Vézelay), 56 (Saulieu), and Oursel, *La miniature du XIIe siècle*, pl. 1 (Dijon MS 30, Psalter of Robert, Flagellation), 48 (Dijon, MS 132, Jerome and Gregory).

242. Oursel, *La miniature du XIIe siècle*, pl. 22 (Gregory, Moralia in Job).

243. That the strict convention of the three-quarters head in the Parma manuscript replaces a more varied older practice in Cluny is evident from the drawing in B.N.N.A. lat. 2390 (Fig. 63), with its four distinct positions of the head; the ruler is in three-quarters, the executioners—the most active figures—are in strict profile, near profile and strict frontal postures.

244. Oursel, *La miniature du XIIe siècle*, pl. 12.

245. Porter, *Romanesque Sculpture*, ill. 14; cf. also ill. 122, La Charité, the angel on the lintel addressing the shepherds.

246. Cf. the Gotha-Nuremberg Codex Aureus (Metz, *Das goldene Evangelienbuch*, pls. 67-69), also the Munich pericope book, lat. 15713, from Regensburg (G. Swarzenski, *Regensburger Malerei*, pl. XXII).

247. Porter, *Romanesque Sculpture*, ill. 16.

248. Cf. Porter, *Romanesque Sculpture*, ills. 34a, 35, 46 (Vézelay), 55 (Saulieu), 77, 78 (Autun), 105 (Montceaux-l'Étoile), 115 (La Charité, Transfiguration).

249. Oursel, *La miniature du XIIe siècle*, pl. 33 (Dijon MS 641). The same form appears earlier in Cluny in B.N.N.A. lat. 2390 (Fig. 63).

and sculptors infused movement into the primitive figures by contrasting positions of the limbs, sharply turned from each other. It is an essential factor in the expressive force of the tympana and capitals of Vézelay and Autun.

Passing from the style to object-forms, we note that the monastic costume of the Parma Codex is pervasive in Burgundian sculpture of the twelfth century. Saints Paul and Anthony, Benedict and others, are represented in Cluniac clothes.[250] Even the fashions peculiar to the Parma Codex, the openings and ties of the sides and tail of the robe, can be matched in Burgundian art.[251]

The second artist, too, has connections with Burgundian works outside the current of Italo-Byzantine forms, especially in his ornament. Some of these similarities may be due, however, to the wider diffusion of such motifs from Italian art. The quatrefoils of the entablature above Gotiscalc appear on the upper band of a capital in Cluny.[252] The great rosette on the crown of the dome is like the repeated theme on the archivolts of the side doors of Vézelay[253] and on a relief in the Cluny museum.[254] Even the acanthus capital has parallels in this region, as on the early altar of Avenas;[255] and the polygonal towers, with triple openings on each story, and the large dome over a polygonal drum, correspond to the forms of Burgundian Romanesque buildings, including Cluny itself. Another little detail of this miniature, the voluted projection from the bishop's throne, is found on the throne of Christ on a tympanum from Anzy-le-Duc and on other Burgundian works.[256] It is neither Byzantine nor Italian, and this by itself supports our idea of the painter's indigenous character.

From these parallels between the paintings of the Parma Codex and other Burgundian Romanesque works, it is clear that however different the individual styles of native artists in this fertile generation were, they had many elements in common. Certain of the motifs—Germanic and Italian—of the two Cluniac painters must have existed in Burgundy by 1100 and belonged to a stratum of styles that underlay the varied Burgundian art of the first third of the twelfth century. The newer Byzantine figural types do not seem to have entered sculpture, however, until late in the second quarter of the century, as at Nevers, St.-Menoux, St.-Julien-de-Jonzy, Charlieu, etc.; though in earlier stone carving an older Byzantine factor may be surmised, as in the balanced asymmetrical stance of the angels of the tympanum of Anzy-le-Duc. The sculptors of the first generation of the twelfth century, native pupils of stonemasons and carvers of capitals, were more occupied with mastery of relief, and perhaps as laymen were less affected by the monastic outlook and the Italian tradition. The painterly aspect of the Italianate style, the patterned highlights of the face and costume, had little interest for sculptors striving to create relief and movement; but the aspects of naturalness and volume in those foreign figures must have supported the new demand for the tangible and weighty in all representation.

In the capitals of Cluny we meet a third kind of art, which seems more truly native; it is connected with a large school of Burgundian works, including several of the highest power and finesse.

Perhaps the fuller humanity realized in this school was also expressed in Cluniac painting,

250. Cf. Porter, *Romanesque Sculpture*, ills. 36, 43 (Vézelay), 56 (Saulieu).

251. Porter, *Romanesque Sculpture*, ill. 91 (St. Paul-de-Varax, Ain).

252. Porter, *Romanesque Sculpture*, ill. 9; the same quatrefoil appears in 1650, fols. 8, 35v, 36v, 81, sometimes alternating with X's and other simple geometrical forms (fols. 10v-11, 13v ff.)—see our Figs. 25x,y, 26a-e; it is found in just such combinations in wall-paintings, as at Ternand (Deschamps and Thibout, *La peinture murale*, pp. 32, 35, figs. 3, 4). Cf. also the rosettes on the frame of the north door of the Cluniac priory church of Paray-le-Monial.

253. Porter, *Romanesque Sculpture*, ills. 50, 51.

254. Porter, *Romanesque Sculpture*, ill. 10. Cf. also the relief in Charlieu, *ibid.*, ill. 16.

255. Porter, *Romanesque Sculpture*, ill. 15.

256. Now in the Musée Hiéron at Paray-le-Monial (Porter, *Romanesque Sculpture*, ills. 98, 99); it appears also on the tympanum still in place at Anzy, *ibid.*, ill. 97. Cf. also the examples at Avenas (ills. 11, 12) and Perrecy-les-Forges (ill. 84). In his imaginary restoration of the Cluny tympanum, Prof. Conant has given the throne of Christ voluted ends (turning up and inward rather than outward as on Joseph's seat on the relief at Charlieu, and unlike the form at Anzy); see Joan Evans, *Cluniac Art of the Romanesque Period*, fig. 20 and note 228 above. It is possible that the Burgundian form is a reduced vestige of the Byzantine lyre-shaped throne; cf. the evangelist's portrait in the Roman manuscript, Florence, Laur. Plut. 17.27 (Garrison, *Studies*, II, fig. 22, p. 38), with S-curved foliate profile.

but did not emerge in the Parma manuscript—an exceptional work destined for a ruler in emulation of the richness of imperial gifts.

The capitals of Cluny, I believe, owe their greater freedom and naturalness to the fact that they were made by lay artists, working together with builders in marble and stone. This vigorous art of sculpture is nearer to folk life, as appears elsewhere in Burgundy in the violence and frankness of its imagery, yet it embodies also the prescribed content of religious thought; in rendering the subjects in stone it is more deeply personal, often ecstatic and exalted. The Burgundian sculptor, drawing on a wider field of imagination and experience and on other sources of feeling than did the disciplined monk in the Cluniac scriptorium, creates a more complete image of the religious and social situation. In Cîteaux, which was closer than Cluny to new stirrings in social and economic life, the same advanced forms penetrate the scriptorium, although by the second decade of the twelfth century there appear in the Cistercian manuscripts the Byzantine types that had been adopted earlier in Cluny.

CHAPTER XIII

THE DATE OF THE PARMA CODEX

I HAVE assumed in all the preceding discussion that the manuscript was written and illustrated about 1100 or at the very beginning of the twelfth century, but I have offered no evidence for this dating. Given the style of Hand A and the ornament and script of the codex, I believe that few if any students would doubt this judgment. The ornament by itself might even suggest a still earlier time because of the parallels in Ottonian art. The figures, the initials, and certain motifs of the borders occur in Paris, Bibl. Nat. lat. 1087, which is clearly of the second half of the eleventh century and shows a script with older forms than those of the Parma Codex (Fig. 41).[257] Only the style of Hand B, of a type that in Italy ranges over a longer period, from the last third of the eleventh century and throughout the twelfth, leads us to consider the possibility of a later date. (An Italian work of that kind, the painted wood panel of the Last Judgment in the Vatican Pinacoteca, has been dated by different scholars in the late eleventh century and in the thirteenth.)[258] We have seen that the frescoes of Berzé-la-Ville, after having been taken for works of about 1100, were judged by Grabar to be of the second half of the twelfth century. In the Parma manuscript the two styles are associated with the same ornament of the frames and were undoubtedly done at the same time.[259]

The lack of securely dated painting from Cluny makes it difficult to fix narrow limits of time for these miniatures with certainty. But for comparison with the script and the ornament we can turn to what may be considered a dated work from Cluny: the annals written in front of the cartulary, Paris Bibl. Nat. Nouv. Acq. lat. 1497. The cartulary assembles in an order corresponding roughly to their order in time the charters of Cluny, grouped in sections identified with the abbots, from Berno to Hugo, under whom the original charters were written. The work of transcription, which filled three volumes with copies of documents dating from 910 to about 1120, proceeded slowly from the middle of the eleventh century and was done by many scribes.[260] In the foreword (fol. 7), one of them says that he undertook to compose the cartulary at the urging of the venerable Odilo ("patris Odilonis venerabilis instancia"); and in fact the oldest writing and decoration of the cartulary—ornamented initials that were probably not in the original documents—resemble the art of the first half of the eleventh century and cannot be far in time from 1049, when Odilo died.[261]

Prefaced to the collection is a history of Cluny in annalistic form, which was written in a style so close to that of the Parma Codex that one might regard them as by the same hand (Fig. 66).

257. I have already remarked (in note 12) that the script of 1087 is by the rubricator of 1650, who is evidently of a generation older than the scribe who wrote the text of the Parma Codex. The presence of the same kind of initial in Paris, B.N.N.A. lat. 1455, which was written not long after the middle of the 11th century, supports our dating of Parma 1650.

258. For the late 11th-century dating, see D. Redig de Campos, "Sopra una tavola sconosciuta del secolo undecimo rappresentante il Giudizio Universale," *Atti della Pontificia Accademia Romana d'Archeologia*, Rendiconti, XI, 1935, pp. 139-156, and the same writer's article: "Eine unbekannte Darstellung des jüngsten Gerichts aus dem 11. Jahrhundert," *Zeitschrift für Kunstgeschichte*, V, 1936, pp. 124-133. For the dating in the 13th century see W. Paeseler in *Kunstgeschichtliches Jahrbuch der Bibliothek Hertziana*, II, 1938, pp. 313-394; Garrison, *Studies*, III, 1, p. 13. For a color reproduction, see Calvesi, *Treasures of the Vatican*, Geneva, 1962, p. 20.

259. Nordenfalk, while recognizing the significance of the ornament for the common date of the two hands (*Romanesque Painting*, p. 190), has placed the work of the Ildefonsus painter in the "second half of the eleventh century" on p. 188 and the Colophon master "ca. 1100(?)" on page 189 in the captions of the illustrations; and on page 190 he has noted that the latter has the "same characteristic style of figure painting as that of Valenciennes MS 501," which is dated "ca. 1140" on p. 187. On the ornament see note 117 above.

260. On the cartulary, which consists of B.N.N.A. lat. 1497(A), 1498(B), and 2262(C), see Bruel, *Recueil des Chartes de l'abbaye de Cluny*, I, pp. xivff. See also L. Delisle, *Fonds de Cluni*, pp. 230, 231. The order of writing does not correspond strictly to the order of the dates of the charters; there are many belated insertions. The annals preceding the oldest charters were begun when the cartulary was already far advanced.

261. Cf. N.A. lat. 1497, fols. 7v, 164v, and *passim*, and 1498, fol. 4 (initial A); for examples of the earlier and later styles of initial, see Bruel, *Recueil des chartes*, I, facsimile I (1497, fol. 83v) and II (1498, fol. 36).

This scribe wrote the numbers of the years from 910 to 1108 and the entries of events up to and including 1088, all in the same ink (fols. 1-2v). For the earlier part he must have had before him an older text or at least a model that contained entries for certain years; most of the years in his list are accompanied by blanks, while the memorable years up to 1088 are followed by lengthy paragraphs for which space had to be reserved in advance. Where the events were added after the writing of the numerals and required more than a single line, as for 1119 (death of Pope Gelasius II and election of Calixtus II), the numbers 1120 to 1124 (fol. 3) had to be erased and rewritten lower on the page. Another hand, with later forms, supplied the events of 1095 and 1096;[262] and a third scribe recorded the death of abbot Hugo in 1109 and the succession by Pontius in a long paragraph written in a style of letters which is apparently of that time, and more developed in the sense of twelfth century writing than the script of the entry of 1088.[263] We are able to say, then, that the style of the first annalist-scribe dates from 1088—or, at the latest, just before 1095, if we wish to allow for the possibility that the scribe, soon after he had commenced, in 1094 or 1095, the annals for the whole period up to 1108, was for some reason unavailable for the entry of 1095. It seems more probable that, like other writers of annals and calendars during this period, the scribe in 1088, anticipating later entries, added numerals for the twenty years up to 1108.[264] The composition of the annals in 1088, when the scribe noted the beginning of the new church ("Fundatio huius basilicae," ii Kl. Oct.) might have been connected with the great enterprise of building.[265]

The initial A heading these annals (Fig. 66) could be placed, without incongruity, in the Parma manuscript and the Cluny lectionary (Fig. 57). The forms are identical; yellow replaces the gold of the more sumptuous manuscripts and the green and blue background is maintained. Small differences in the common type of script suggest that of the three books, the lectionary is the oldest and the Parma Codex the most recent, although the ornament is in essence the same. The script of the lectionary is the simplest, clearest, most stable and regular in form—the classic writing of this school. In the Parma Codex, which has a similar clarity, the letters are slightly more articulated and fractured; and the first hand of the annals can be interpolated between them. A characteristic of this group and a sign of the general taste for distinctness, balance, and a simple order is the use of the majuscule L in the minuscule writing. It is anticipated in Cluny in some older manuscripts of the eleventh century, Bibl. Nat. lat. 15176 and 1087.

We cannot say how long such a script was practiced, nor what range of difference between new and old forms was possible at the same moment in a large scriptorium where monks of different ages were at work, often on the same books. Would a scribe who had learned to write in a book hand in 1090 have changed his forms appreciably by 1110? In the Parma manuscript the rubricator has an older style than the main scribe, and is more obviously of the eleventh century. A study of all the surviving manuscripts of this period from Cluny, taking into account the variants in spelling, abbreviations, stroke structure, and the forms of the undecorated majuscule writing and initials, might disclose an order in the fine variations, a drift in calligraphy, that would help us to fix the order of works more securely.[266]

262. These are written over erased matter, either because the original entry was incorrect or in order to make space for a longer entry at 1095 and a second one at 1096. The two entries record the consecration of the high altar of the new church of Cluny by Pope Urban II and the First Crusade to Jerusalem.

263. It is close in style to the page with the office for Odilo, which was added to B.N. lat. 1087 (fol. 112v) early in the 12th century. See note 12 above.

264. The annals were continued up to 1215.

265. That the first hand of the annals wrote before 1109, the date of Hugo's death, is confirmed by his entry for 1049 on Hugo's accession: "Nunc in presenti, ut decet, offitii sui ministerium adimplet."

266. I note, without insisting on the dependability of the criterion, that in Parma 1650 the use of uncial s as a final letter (distinguished from the older use of the suspended s in final "us," etc.) instead of the minuscule form, is more frequent than in N.A. lat. 2246 and increases toward the end of the manuscript; in N.A. lat. 1497, fols. 1, 2 (the first hand of the annals), this element approaches in frequency the count in Parma 1650; in N.A. lat. 2246 (in the original part) it is lacking on many pages and is exceptional in the rest. The same relationship holds for the use of the uncial form of d beside the minuscule.

If the paintings in the Italo-Byzantine style in the Parma Codex, Bibl. Nat. N.A. 2246, and Berzé-la-Ville are to be regarded as works of the same period of a decade or longer during Hugo's rule, comparison of their common features has yielded no compelling ground for placing them in a definite order of time. Another painting in this style, the miniature in Montreal (Fig. 50), is associated with a script that seems as early as the writing in the Cluny lectionary. One might judge the Parma Codex to be later than the lectionary, since the painter of the presentation page (Colorplate II) not only stiffens and coarsens the style of the lectionary miniatures, but employs elements of the native Romanesque which are lacking in the lectionary and in Berzé-la-Ville. But these two works need not be regarded as the first of their kind; they may continue the Italo-Byzantine practice after the time of its absorption by the Colophon painter.

CHAPTER XIV

THE TEXT

THE Parma Codex belongs to a distinct class of copies of the Ildefonsus text.[267] All the manuscripts of this family contain the prologue-colophon of the copy that was written in Spain by Gómez, a monk of Albailde, for Gotiscalc, bishop of Le Puy, during the latter's visit to Spain in 951. This copy, now preserved in Paris (Bibl. Nat. MS lat. 2855), is the ancestor of a group of manuscripts with the same text, executed between the eleventh and thirteenth centuries.[268] Like the Gómez copy, these manuscripts are incomplete, lacking the last two chapters; they share with it several variant readings of the original text that are not found in the early Spanish copies.[269]

Among the descendants of the Le Puy Codex, one can distinguish a subclass of which the Parma Ildefonsus is a member. This class is defined by the following peculiarities (among others):

a) The prologue of Gómez is at the end of the text, not at the beginning as in the autograph version in Paris, Bibl. Nat. lat. 2855.

b) For "Gomes" is written "Gomesanus."

c) The Spanish "Albaildense" becomes "Abba hyldense," creating a new place name: "hyldensis."

This sub-class consists of the following manuscripts:

Paris, Bibl. Nat., Nouv. Acq. lat. 1455, eleventh century, from Cluny
Paris, Bibl. de l'Arsenal, 371, eleventh century, from Cluny
Paris, Bibl. de l'Arsenal, 372, eleventh century, from St.-Benoît-sur-Loire
Paris, Bibl. Nat., lat. 2359, early twelfth century, from St.-Martin-des-Champs
Parma, Bibl. Pal. 1650, about 1100, from Cluny
Dijon, Bibl. Publique, 232, end of twelfth century (?), from Cîteaux
Madrid, Bibl. Nac., 10087, about 1200, from Toledo

Within this group a further subdivision can be made: in Parma 1650, Paris. Bibl. Nat. lat. 1455, Arsenal 371 and Madrid 10087, "diebus certis" in the colophon is read "diebus ceptis"—a community of error of which the import will become apparent presently.

The relationship of these manuscripts to each other is instructive for the history of the Parma Codex and its Cluniac origin. Three of them can be shown to have come from Cluny;[270] two (Bibl. Nat. lat. 2359, Arsenal 372) are from priories reformed by Cluny; one is from the

267. For the manuscripts of this text, see Vicente Blanco García, *San Ildefonso*.

268. For the Gómez copy and its descendants, see Blanco García, *San Ildefonso*, pp. 11-13, 40-43, 53ff.; Delisle, *Le Cabinet des Manuscrits de la Bibl. nat.*, I, pp. 516ff. Though Parma 1650 was known to Blanco García through its mention by Manitius (see note 18 above), he has not collated it; four other Cluniac copies in French libraries, noted in this section, seem to have escaped his attention.

269. The incompleteness is not due to the loss of pages of MS 2855, but to the copying of an incomplete model in Spain in 951. The same concluding chapters are missing also in two Spanish copies of the 11th century, Silos 5 (dated 1059) and Madrid, Academia de la Historia, Aem. 47, from San Millán de la Cogolla, as noted by Blanco García, p. 161. On the margin of the last page of the text in B.N. lat. 2855 (fol. 159), are written in a script of the early 12th century: "hic des(unt) octo folia. Quia enim," followed by an erasure. "Quia enim" are the words that follow in the complete text. In two of the manuscripts descended from the Gómez copy, Madrid 10087 and Paris, B.N. lat. 2833 (see Appendix II), the missing chapters have been supplied from a Spanish source—in the second manuscript perhaps through a French copy.

Note that the doxology at the end of the text of Ildefonsus in Parma 1650—"per numquam finienda secula seculorum, amen"—is not found in 2855, but occurs in 10087, B.N.N.A. lat. 1455, and Arsenal 371. Blanco, who, on p. 37, notes its absence in 2855, mistakenly attributes it to this manuscript in the collation on p. 161, note to line 7.

270. B.N.N.A. lat. 1455, Arsenal 371 and Parma 1650. Though Arsenal 371 is bound with a manuscript containing a calendar of St.-Mesmin near Orléans, the ornamented initials of the Ildefonsus texts are of the same style as those of the Cluniac scriptorium. N.A. lat. 1455 came to Paris from Cluny and can be identified with no. 376 in the catalogue of the Cluny library of about 1160. See note 272 below.

Burgundian abbey of Cîteaux;[271] and we shall see that the Spanish example, Madrid 10087, has been copied from the Parma Codex.

Study of the text in these manuscripts makes it clear that although Bibl. Nat. Nouv. Acq. lat. 1455 was produced earlier than the Parma Codex and was still at Cluny when the latter was written—since it is listed in the catalogue of the Cluny library drawn up in the middle of the twelfth century[272]—its text was not adhered to by the scribe of the Parma Codex. They differ not only in readings of single words and phrases, but also in the rubrics and chapter divisions. The Parma Codex has a purer spelling and reflects in many details the effort to produce a better text. The inadequacy of Bibl. Nat. Nouv. Acq. lat. 1455 was recognized early, and a corrector of this manuscript has changed some of the readings to accord with the improved text of the Parma Codex (or its model).[273] With respect to this editing of the text, Arsenal 371 seems to lie between the two.[274] During the eleventh and early twelfth centuries there was evidently much interest at Cluny in the book of Ildefonsus, which was copied there several times and reworked. If the Le Puy Codex was the ancestor of all these versions, we must assume that there were intermediaries or collateral models that have been lost; all the Cluny copies contain significant deviations from the Le Puy manuscript. The Parma Codex itself departs from the other Cluniac copies, while agreeing with them in the distinctive family details. Or we must suppose a considerable alertness and individuality in the scribes who changed the text of the model according to their feeling for the language.

But the Parma Codex is unique in the degree of transformation. Not only is it distinct in the text, but among the French manuscripts of Ildefonsus it is the only one that possesses a series of full-page illustrations.[275] It is a luxury manuscript designed for an august recipient, with ornamented frames on every page and with lavish use of gold, silver and purple. The revision of the text is one sign among several that the Parma book was an object of special effort, and not a copy like the others, which were designed for devotional reading and often combined with various texts on the Virgin.

271. B.N. lat. 2359 has an *ex-libris* of the Cluniac priory of St.-Martin-des-Champs. Arsenal 372 is very close in text to Arsenal 371 and is followed like the latter by Fulbert's sermon "In ortu almae Virginis Mariae." A note in the manuscript states that it belonged to the abbey of St.-Benoît-sur-Loire, a monastery that had been reformed by Cluny.

272. Under abbot Hugo III (1158-1161); see Delisle, *Fonds de Cluni*, pp. 337ff., no. 376. The manuscript is described by Delisle, pp. 96-101.

273. E.g., the reading "viviturum" in Spanish manuscripts (Blanco, *San Ildefonso*, p. 61), changed to "victurum" in the Parma Codex, fol. 8v, is repeated in 1455, where a corrector of the same period has written "victurum" over the original "viviturum." The corrector's mark for a missing h (⊦) appears in both 1650 and 1455.

274. The format of 371 is close to that of 1650: 220 by 153 mm. and 21 long lines; compare with 1650: 230 by 160 mm. and 19 long lines. The historical note found in 1455 and other manuscripts after the "amen" of the colophon, "Ipsis diebus igitur obiit Galleciacensis Rex Ranimirus," is omitted in 371 and 1650, but appears in Madrid 10087. It is inserted in 2359, fol. 115.

275. For another illustrated French copy, but with small miniatures, see Appendix II on Paris, B.N. lat. 2833.

CHAPTER XV

THE MADRID ILDEFONSUS, MS. 10087

ONE other manuscript in the same class of copies is richly illustrated, the Madrid Codex, Bibl. Naç. 10087 (M). Though written in Spain around 1200, it includes the historic colophon of Gómez and was surely copied directly from a Cluniac manuscript, for it not only contains the exceptional features that distinguish the smaller Cluniac subgroup from the other French members of the same family,[276] but several of its illustrations clearly depend on the pictures in Parma. Where its text differs from the Cluniac model, we recognize a Spanish addition or correction, as in the rendering of Spanish names that had been Gallicized in the French manuscripts (Galitie for Galliciae, e(x) Spania for ex Hispania). The two chapters (XI, XII) that were missing in the Le Puy copy and in the Cluniac descendants of the latter, have been supplied in the Madrid Codex from an old Toledo manuscript.[277] An inscription of the early fourteenth century on fol. 1 indicates that the Madrid Codex belonged then to the library of the chaplains of the confraternity of the choir of Toledo Cathedral. It is likely that this copy was done in Toledo itself, and that the Parma Codex had come to Toledo before 1200.

Although we do not have to concern ourselves with the miniatures of the Madrid Codex for the problems of Cluniac art in 1100, they pertain to the history of the Parma miniatures as significant copies of the latter. To compare the two series is to see more clearly both the character of the early miniatures and the process of conversion of Romanesque forms between 1100 and 1200.

In several miniatures the Spanish artist has held closely to his model, like the scribe who, conscious of the importance of the illustrations, adapted the spacing of his copy to the model in order to maintain the original relationship of text and pictures. In the Madrid Codex, which is like the Parma Codex in format and number of leaves, the eighteen lines per page approximate the nineteen in the older manuscript, and its majuscules and initials correspond broadly to those of the model.[278]

276. Beside the distinctive features of the Cluniac subclass listed above (p. 62) and the "diebus ceptis" of 1650, 1455, and 371, it has the doxology at the end of the Ildefonsus text which is missing in 2855 and appears in those three manuscripts. Among other variants shared with 1650, I note "victurum" (instead of "viviturum"), "cum Deo patre" (for "cum patre"), and the omission of a line from Malachi 3:1, as in 1650, fol. 36 (and in some old Spanish manuscripts) but not in 2855 (Blanco, *San Ildefonso*, p. 88). I note, however, that the scribe of Madrid 10087 must have had at least two French copies of the Ildefonsus manuscript before him, for in some respects his text is closer to that of 1455. As in the latter, the reference to the death of Ranimir at the end of the colophon (found also in 2855) is written in red capitals.

277. According to Blanco, *San Ildefonso*, pp. 16, 17, it was either the Florence manuscript of 1067 or the Toledo codex of the 9th century, both of which were written in Toledo.

278. Madrid 10087 (old numbers: C.15.14 and Hh175) has i + 112 leaves, 13 cm. by 18 cm., long lines, pencil rulings. There were originally 115 leaves, according to an old inscription, "CXV fojas," on the last page. A leaf or two leaves are missing between fols. 4v and 5. The painting on fol. 4 is 103 by 130 mm. (cf. with 1650: 125 by 185 mm.). In the initials, which are of a foliate type familiar ca. 1200, the background is strewn with a motif of three little tangent circles that might have been suggested by the trefoils in 1650.

The manuscript has been described and catalogued by J. Dominguez Bordona, *Códices Miniados Españoles*, p. 190, no. LII; *idem*, *Spanish Illuminated Manuscripts*, Florence, New York, 1930, I, pl. 48A (reproducing fols. 104v, 111v); *idem*, *Manuscritos con Pinturas*, Madrid, 1933, I, p. 353, no. 898, fig. 296 (fol. 9v); *Stora Spanska Mästare*, National-museum, Stockholm, 1959, pp. 29, 30, no. 5 (edited by Carl Nordenfalk, who observed the resemblance to Parma 1650).

I list the miniatures and initials in Madrid 10087 and note the correspondences with Parma 1650 (P); for the description of the latter, see pp. 73ff., Appendix I. The pagination follows the notes that I made in 1931; these do not agree with the page numbers in the Spanish publications, but it should be remarked that there are two sets of such numbers in the manuscript itself.

fol. 1–Initial and incipit of the Julian Vita (P, fol. 2).
1v–"sui temporis clarus. . . ."
4–Ildefonsus leaves his parents for the monastery, against their wishes.
4v–Ildefonsus receives the monastic robe.
9v–Ildefonsus, kneeling, prays to the enthroned Virgin (P, fol. 9v).
10–"Domina mea" (P, fol. 10).
12v–Ildefonsus argues with "Juvenianus" (P, fol. 12v).
13–Audi tu (P, fol. 13).
16–Ildefonsus argues with Helvidius (P, fol. 15v).
16v–Ad me . . (P, fol. 16); in 10087, "Audi ergo, et tu, Helvidi," is on fol. 15v, preceding the miniature, and the initial A, with decoration, is shifted to fol. 16v: "Ad me adtende . . .").
23–Ildefonsus and the Jews (P, fol. 22—a very close copy).
23v–"Quid dicis, Iudee . . ." (P, fol. 22v).
40–"Quid egisti, dñe" (P, fol. 45, where this text follows a

Of the fourteen miniatures in Madrid (Figs. 70-84) seven are of subjects from the life of Saint Ildefonsus that are not illustrated in Parma, though based on the common text.[279] The Spanish artist was more concerned with the great native saint of Toledo, the French with the theologian and his work. While copying from his model the full-page scenes representing Ildefonsus and the Virgin (Fig. 72, cf. Fig. 3), the bishop disputing with his heretical and Jewish opponents (Figs. 74-76, cf. Figs. 4-6), and performing the mass (Fig. 83, cf. Fig. 2), the painter has omitted the frontispiece page of Julian, the Christ in majesty, and the smaller pictures of the prophets and patriarchs. He has added scenes illustrating the life of the saint recounted by Julian and Cixila: Ildefonsus' departure from his family to become a monk (Figs. 70, 71), his entry into the monastery, the miracle of the Virgin presenting him with a chasuble (Fig. 82), the episodes concerning Saint Leocadia and king Receswinth, and the burial of Ildefonsus (Figs. 79, 80, 84).

On the pages preceding the colophon of Gómez are two paintings which I take to be illustrations of the colophon. One shows an angel addressing Ildefonsus (Fig. 77), presumably based on the idea of the author's inspiration by angels in writing the book;[280] and the second represents Gómez offering his copy to the bishop Gotiscalc (Fig. 78).

For one of the added scenes the painter has used as a model an omitted scene from the Parma Codex.[281] He has also applied single elements from the copied pages to several of the new miniatures.[282] In copying two of the scenes of argument, he has confused them, exchanging the details of the dispute with Helvidius and those of the dispute with Jovinianus.[283]

He has framed the scenes in double borders of gold and silver, but without the ornament of his model, and he has set the figures on a gold ground in arched constructions as in Parma. In only one scene, the added picture of Ildefonsus leaving his family (Fig. 70), has he introduced a specifically Spanish form in the architecture: a building with a horseshoe arch and pointed crenelations that recalls the old Puerta de Visagra in Toledo. But in copying the buildings from his model, he has reduced their open skeletal aspect, giving them a massiveness typical of southern regions where there is a strong Islamic influence.

Yet the general aspect of the Parma paintings has guided the Spanish artist in certain of the scenes that he has had to invent; they are framed and designed in the same way, and in Fig. 71 the figures are raised above the ground level, suspended in space as in Cluny.

It was possible for the Spanish artist to reproduce so much of the earlier form because his own style, while in a sense more naturalistic, was still bound to Romanesque conventions.

Nevertheless, it is easy to see the changes produced in the character of the original miniatures by the Spanish copyist as a consistent transformation that rests on the intervening development

painting of Ildefonsus arguing with two Jews).
48v–"Omnia quae habet pater. . . ."
67v–"Veni, sancte Gabriel."
85–"Quia generatio filii."
100v–Angel addresses Ildefonsus.
101–Gómez presents the book to Gotiscalc (P, fol. 102v).
101v–Ego quidem Gomesanus (P, fol. 103–the colophon of 951).
103v–Ecce dapes (P, fol. 105v–the life of Ildefonsus by Elladius, *sc.* Cixila).
109v–Ildefonsus cuts the veil of St. Leocadia.
110–Ildefonsus at the altar, followed by the king.
110v–Ildefonsus addresses two monks (P, fol. 1v).
111–Ildefonsus receives the robe from the Virgin; beside her stand two virgins, who are mentioned in Cixila's account of the miracle.
111v–Ildefonsus performs the mass (P, fol. 4).
112–Burial of Ildefonsus.

279. These are on fols. 4, 4v, 100v, 109v, 110, 111, 112.

280. An old inscription on fol. 100v underneath the painting reads: "de angelo vide in prologo sequenti." It was suggested perhaps by the passage in which Gómez says that Ildefonsus in defeating the heretics and Jews "non solum a stipulatione angelorum et hominum sed etiam demonum prolata confessione iugulavit." It may be compared with the scene of the angel and Daniel in Parma (Fig. 16).

281. Cf. in Madrid, fol. 110 (Fig. 80), the three heads in the upper building with those in Parma, fol. 40v–the prophet Micah (Fig. 17).

282. Cf. the architecture of M, the miracle of the Virgin (Fig. 82), with that of P (Fig. 3); and of M, burial of Ildefonsus (Fig. 84), with P (Figs. 1, 2). Note also in M (Fig. 80) that the diapered ornament of the bishop's chasuble is like the ornament of the altar in P (Fig. 2).

283. In Fig. 75 the Spanish painter shows Helvidius clutching his beard, like Jovinianus in P (Fig. 4); the architecture in M, fol. 16 corresponds to that in P, fol. 12v, while M, Fig. 74, resembles the forms in P, Fig. 5. The copyist gives Jovinianus on fol. 12v the shrub that belongs to Helvidius on P, fol. 15v. On M, fol. 15v, the scribe has miscopied the name "Elvidii" in the opening text, as ELIVDV, although he has written "Elbidium" in the line above.

during the twelfth century and includes Italo-Byzantine forms.[284] While the French Romanesque artist works with strongly accented inner lines of the figures and buildings as a closely bound system or net, the Spanish painter thinks in terms of casually streaked folds on large masses of color. He aims at a still clearer, spot-like form; the articulations in the Parma miniatures have been simplified; the buildings, like the figures, are distinct, silhouetted areas of color.

These figures are more definitely tied to the frame and the ground line by similarity and contact. Where the older artist places the sloping diagonal feet across the lower border, in the later paintings the feet rest on the border as the imaginary ground of the building. In a similar way, the outlines of the figures in Madrid are parallel to or touch the architectural setting; in Parma, they cross the architecture and often seem independent of it.

The mass of the figure as a whole is simpler, with a single dominant axis. In the Parma manuscript some figures have broken, zigzag, angular forms; or if they are simple as a whole, the large form is less vivid than a particular part or a set of active folds.

These differences may be discerned also in the gestures, which are so important a means of expression in the Parma Codex. I have noted the asymmetrical, indented, angular, and crossing forms produced by these gestures in the older manuscript. In the Spanish copy the same gestures have been restrained and are adapted to the compactness of the body as a whole (Fig. 70).

In general, the model is more schematic, more systematized in form; but also more forceful through the network and thrust of lines. The less pronounced and freer, cursive drawing of the Spanish artist is accompanied by a further sobering of expression. The change is not only a matter of the painter's slighter power of realizing a content of feeling; it has also to do with a general shift of attitude which appears in monumental sculpture as well: an idea of the qualities of the human being as a physical organism with an order and harmony of its own has begun to stabilize the figure and restrains the Romanesque intensity of posture, whether active or rigid.

284. Cf. especially the Virgin in Fig. 72.

CHAPTER XVI

THE PURPOSE OF THE PARMA CODEX

For whom was the Parma Codex made? Why was the uncommon text of Ildefonsus given so luxurious a form with so many pictures that were probably first designed for this copy?[285] Unlike other medieval manuscripts of this sumptuous kind, it contains no reference to the maker or recipient either in a colophon or an image of presentation. This fact is all the more remarkable since the donor thought it fitting to provide two miniatures to illustrate the colophon of his model—pictures that do not occur with the original colophon in Paris, Bibl. Nat. lat. 2855 nor in other copies made at Cluny.[286] The two miniatures show a scribe writing the old copy 150 years before and presenting it to a bishop who apparently was no figure in Cluny's history. It may be that the Parma manuscript was accidentally damaged or that a colophon page has been removed. The first two leaves (fols. i, ii), which belong to the first gathering of the book, are blank, as is also the recto of the third leaf (fol. 1 in the present pagination),[287] on the back of which is the miniature that prefaces Julian's life of Ildefonsus (fol. 1v). Besides, the last written page of the codex, fol. 111, is not part of a quire, but is joined to the blank leaf, fol. 112, to form a union; it is written by another hand than the rest in a somewhat later artificial style that reproduces the forms of the original Cluniac scribe (Fig. 36).[288] There is reason to believe that this page was added elsewhere than in Cluny: it omits the final sentence of the text of Elladius' (*sc.* Cixila's) life of Ildefonsus, a doxology that appears in older copies of this text written at Cluny;[289] and it differs from the corresponding passages in those copies in nine places,[290] whereas the preceding page, fol. 110v, agrees strictly with the other Cluniac manuscripts.[291] One can make many guesses to explain how the beginning and end of this lavishly prepared book came to be bare and mute as they are, and the last written page so anomalous. But lacking internal evidence, we shall try to learn something positive about the origin of the book from its later history.

285. There was until recently another illustrated manuscript of Ildefonsus on the Virginity of Mary, in the Lazaro Collection in Madrid. It is described in the catalogue: *Manuscritos con Pinturas*, ed. by J. Dominguez Bordona, I, p. 513, no. 1222, as a work of Toledan art of the late 12th or early 13th century, with nine drawings of the life of Saint Ildefonsus. The one reproduced in fig. 431, p. 514, shows the bishop-saint cutting the veil of Saint Leocadia; the background is an arcade with a central pointed arch. In another publication, *La Colección Lazaro*, Madrid, 2a parte, Madrid, 1927, are reproduced two more pages of this manuscript. One (no. 924) represents Ildefonsus disputing with Helvidius; the two figures are seated under an arcade and are accompanied by eight other figures. The second page (no. 925) shows the Virgin giving the chasuble to Ildefonsus. She *stands* at the right and is followed by four virgins. I have not been able to study the original manuscript or to obtain photographs of the miniatures. I learn from Dr. Helmut Schlunk, director of the German Archaeological Institute in Madrid, that the manuscript had been transferred to the Biblioteca Nacional in 1938, together with other manuscripts of the collection, but was not among those which were returned after the Civil War and must be considered lost.

286. For the illustration of the colophon in Paris, B.N. lat. 2833, see Appendix II.

287. The present numbering of the leaves dates from 1866, according to a note on fol. 1.

288. Although the letter forms, ligatures and abbreviations are the same and the page is framed by the same kind of unornamented triple border as fol. 110v, the appearance of the whole is very different. The words are much more separated and the form ꝛ (for r), which was used by the main scribe throughout only in ligature with a preceding o, occurs here as a first letter of a word and also, without ligature, inside words almost as often as the regular r (the ratio is 7 to 8). Like the more marked separation of words, this is a sign of later date. But how much later than the book and whether it is a restoration of a mutilated page or a replacement of a leaf that had included a colophon are questions I cannot answer. The page has even a modern look because of the isolation of words. As an argument for a date not long after the rest, it should be noted that where a letter has two forms, like the s and d, that occur without a strict rule, the relative frequencies of the two forms are about the same on fol. 111 as on the preceding pages which were written in Cluny.

289. Paris, B.N.N.A. lat. 1455 and Paris, Bibl. de l'Arsenal 371. The sentence reads: "Praestante dño nr̃o ihũ xp̃o qui cum deo patre et scõ spiritu vivit et regit deus per infinita semper scl̄a scl̄orum. Amen." A very similar doxology appears at the end of several sermons of Odilo (Migne, *Pat. lat.*, CXLII, cols. 1005, 1029, etc.).

290. Arsenal 371 and Paris, B.N.N.A. lat. 1455: "Data est" for "danda est"; "fixis" for "fixos"; "tenens" omitted before "permansisti"; "in laudem" for "et laudem"; "et vestimentis gloriae iam in hac vita orneris" for "ex vestimentis ecclesiae iam in hac vitae ornatus eris"; "remansit dei" for "remansit igitur dei"; "promissa" for "donata." Almost all the variant readings in the Parma Codex, fol. 111, agree with the text published in Migne, *Pat. lat.*, XCVI, col. 48, which also omits the doxology.

291. The only difference is the reading "allocuta est voce" where the other two manuscripts say "voce allocuta est."

From the copy in Madrid we have been able to infer that the Parma Codex was in Spain and most likely in Toledo by the end of the twelfth century.[292] Also its later presence in Parma may depend on a connection with Spain. For the great library to which it now belongs was formed in the middle of the eighteenth century when Parma came under Spanish rule. The new duke of Parma, Philip of Bourbon (1749-1765) was the son of Philip of Spain. In 1761, his minister, Du Tillot, called from Rome the scholar, Paolo Paciaudi, to create a library in Parma. From Paciaudi's account we learn that rare manuscripts were then acquired from all parts of Europe and that members of the Spanish Royal house—among them Philip of Spain, prince Fernando and madama Infanta—donated books from their personal collections.[293] But Paciaudi, in his detailed description of the Ildefonsus Codex, says nothing about the donor or the immediate source.[294]

If the manuscript was intended for a Spanish dignitary in Toledo, two names, closely linked with Cluny toward 1100, come to mind. The first is Bernard, the archbishop of Toledo and primate of the Spanish Church; the other is king Alfonso VI.

Bernard of Sédirac (near Agen) was a Cluniac monk, one of those sent to Spain by Hugo at the request of Alfonso VI for the reform of the Spanish monasteries. A trusted counsellor of the king, he became head of the important Cluniac abbey at Sahagun in 1080 and after the conquest of Toledo in 1085 was appointed archbishop at Alfonso's new capital, where he ruled from 1086 until his death in 1122. A letter from Hugo to Bernard speaks of his role in changing the liturgy of the Spanish church from its old Mozarabic forms to the Roman Catholic practice.[295]

The production of a precious manuscript of Ildefonsus, a former bishop of Toledo, as a gift of Cluny to Bernard, would have been particularly appropriate. The provenance of the later copy of the Parma Codex from the Cathedral of Toledo also favors the hypothesis that the Cluniac model had belonged to Bernard. In the Ottonian period in Germany several of the most richly decorated manuscripts were made for great bishops like Gero of Cologne and Egbert of Trier. To these arguments, which are more suggestive than cogent, may be added the fact that the old Cathedral of Toledo was dedicated to Mary and that in the later Gothic building the great east chapel behind the apse was reserved for the relics and cult of Ildefonsus.

It would be surprising, however, that so important a manuscript, if it were in clerical hands for centuries, contained no trace of contemporary or later use in notations, colophons or marks of ownership.[296] In the copy in Madrid are several such inscriptions.[297]

The second possibility, that the manuscript was intended for Alfonso VI, seems to me more plausible, though no conclusive evidence compels one to accept this idea.

At no time were there closer relations between Cluny and the rulers of Castille than during the abbacy of Hugo (1049-1109), under whom the manuscript was produced if our dating is correct.[298] The building of the new church of Cluny, begun in 1088, consecrated in 1095, and nearly com-

292. See pp. 64ff. above.

293. For the history of the library, see Odorici, *Atti e Memorie della R. deputazione di storia patria per le provincie Modenesi e Parmensi*, III, 1867 (cited in note 18 above), pp. 352ff., 360ff., and A. Boselli, "Du Tillot, Paciaudi e la biblioteca di Parma," in *Mélanges Hauvette*, Paris, 1934, pp. 455ff.

294. Parma, Bibl. Palatina MS 1589, vol. IV.

295. On Bernard's career, see Marcelin Defourneaux, *Les français en Espagne aux XIe et XIIe siècles*, Paris, 1949, pp. 17ff. and 33; Hugo's letter to Bernard was published by M. Férotin, "Une lettre inédite de Saint Hugues, Abbé de Cluny, à Bernard d'Agen, archévêque de Tolède (1087)," *Bibliothèque de l'École des Chartes*, LXI, 1900, pp. 339-345.

296. On the second blank leaf, fol. iiv, a non-professional hand of the early 13th century has written: "Confitemini d(omi)no q(uonia)m bonus q(uonia)m in sec(u)lum (misericordia eius)," the first line of Psalm 106. This psalm was read in the service for the dead, and in the old Mozarabic tradition it marked one of the divisions of the five-part psalter, a rare type. An inscription "171" on fol. 1 (and 1v) seems to be a library number of the 18th century.

297. Beside the *ex libris* inscription of the period about 1300 are later writings on the margins of the miniatures describing the scenes.

298. On Cluny and Spain during this period, see E. Sackur, *Die Cluniacenser, bis zur Mitte des elften Jahrhunderts*, Halle, 1894, II, pp. 109-113 (and especially p. 112, note 3); Defourneaux, *Les français en Espagne*, pp. 17-22; L. M. Smith, *Cluny in the Eleventh and Twelfth Centuries*, London, 1930, pp. 219ff.

pleted by the time of Hugo's death in 1109, was made possible by the gifts of Alfonso VI (1072-1109) of Castille and León. He donated to Cluny a large part of the booty won in capturing Toledo from the Moors; and after confirming his father's annual tribute of 1000 gold pieces (mancales), to assure his own place in heaven he agreed to double this tribute for himself and his descendants, and also sent 10,000 talents for the expenses of the rebuilding of the church.[299] At the head of several of the most important Spanish sees and abbeys he appointed Cluniac monks; both Bernard of Sédirac and his predecessor as abbot of Sahagun, the French Cluniac, Robert, were very dear to Alfonso. After Hugo met the king at Burgos in 1090 and received his testament, doubling the annual tribute, the abbot in return wrote statutes expressing and fixing in the liturgy Cluny's gratitude to Alfonso. "No king, in past or present," he wrote, "can be compared to Alfonso, king of Spain, our faithful friend who has done so much for us. In consequence, he shall have a special place in Cluny during his life and after his death. Daily during his life a psalm shall be sung in his honor at the third hour and a collect at high mass. On Easter Thursday thirty poor shall be summoned for him to the mandatum (the washing of feet), and no less than a hundred poor shall be fed out of love for Alfonso. Finally, a place shall be reserved for him daily in the refectory of the monks, as if he were sitting with us, and his share of the meal shall be given to one of the poor in Christ for the salvation of Alfonso's soul, during his life and after his death. In the new church that is being built at his expense, we have given him an altar exclusively for prayers for his soul. His anniversary shall be celebrated like that of the emperor Henry. . . ."[300]

Even in their lifetimes legend had begun to elaborate the story of the friendship of the abbot and the king. Biographers of Hugo wrote soon after his death that Alfonso had been freed from the chains and the prison of his brother Sancho by Hugo's intervention and that this timely aid was the cause of the Spaniard's devotion to the abbot of Cluny. In a vision Saint Peter revealed to a monk of Cluny that he had brought to God Hugo's prayers for Alfonso. Peter also presented himself to the sleeping Sancho and threatened him if he did not free his brother and restore him to his dignity.[301]

Behind the monks' stories lie the historical events that we learn from Spanish sources. When defeated in battle by Sancho during their contest for royal power in 1071, Alfonso was imprisoned and forced to become a monk in the monastery of Sahagun. Alfonso managed to escape to Toledo where he lived as a guest of the Moorish king. Two years later Sancho was treacherously assassinated at Zamora and suspicion fell upon his brother who, in the chronicle of the Cid, is made by the hero to swear three times that he was wholly innocent of the crime. Not long after, Alfonso, now king of Castille and León, had to beg absolution from the church dignitaries, who imposed upon him pilgrimages and spiritual exercises for a grave sin: his incestuous relations with his older sister, Urraca, the ruler of Zamora. Other sources speak of her instigation of crimes useful to Alfonso: the murder of Sancho and the imprisonment for his whole life of her younger brother, García, king of Galicia. She became a nun, and was famous for adorning altars with sacred vestments of gold and silver and precious stones.[302]

Alfonso's sins were known in Cluny. In a charter of his donations to the abbey, he speaks of

299. For the documents, see Bruel, *Recueil des chartes*, IV, nos. 3441, 3509, and Migne, *Pat. lat.*, CLIX, cols. 938, 973, 974. In Bruel, no. 3441 (pp. 551-553), note that it was at Hugo's orders ("tua iussione accepimus") that Alfonso accepted the replacement of the native Spanish liturgy by the foreign Roman Catholic rite, which provoked great popular protest.

300. Migne, *Pat. lat.*, CLIX, cols. 945, 946 (statuta Sancti Hugonis pro Alphonso rege Hispaniarum).

301. Hildebert, Vita Hugonis, Migne, *Pat. lat.*, CLIX, col. 866; the epitome of Hezelo's and Gilo's biographies of Hugo, *ibid.*, col. 912.

302. All this is recounted from Arabic and Latin sources by R. Menéndez Pidal, "Alfonso VI y su hermana la infanta Urraca," *Al-Andalus*, XIII, Madrid, 1948, pp. 157-166, with introduction by E. Lévi-Provençal. In the charter-testament of 1090, in which Alfonso doubles the tribute to Cluny in perpetuity (Bruel, no. 3509), I note that he speaks of saving the souls of his parents, his brothers, his wife and his children, but not of his sister Urraca. Is it possible, however, that the story of incest was built on the pope's disapproval of Alfonso's marriage with Constance of Burgundy in 1079 as incestuous, a marriage that was finally permitted because of Hugo's intervention? (See note 306 below.)

being pressed down by the weight of his sins and fearful at the thought of his crimes.[303] Yet he hoped that the eternal reward would be assured him by his gifts to the apostles Peter and Paul, whose relics he believed to be secretly hid in their basilica at Cluny, and to Hugo and his monks.[304] The abbot Peter the Venerable, traveling in Spain in 1142, heard from a monk in a Cluniac priory an account of Alfonso's soul miraculously carried off from hell by monks of Cluny.[305]

If Alfonso's munificence to a distant Cluny was an expiation of a most unreligious life as well as an expression of gratitude for help in gaining power, he was also bound to Cluny by family ties. In 1079, after the death of his wife, Agnes of Aquitaine, the Spanish king married Constance, daughter of Robert, duke of Burgundy, and the niece of Hugo of Cluny. Urraca, the daughter of this union, married Raymond, a Burgundian prince; their son became Alfonso VII of Castille. Raymond's brother, a former Cluniac monk, was elected pope in 1119 as Calixtus II.[306]

The royal aspect of the Parma Codex, so much like the sumptuous illustrated manuscripts in gold, silver, and purple produced at Reichenau, Regensburg, and Echternach for the German emperors, makes us think that it was a gift to a contemporary monarch.[307] Not only its later presence in Toledo, but the content of the book points to the self-styled "imperator" Alfonso VI as the recipient. The choice of a text, written by an early saintly bishop of Toledo of the same name as the Spanish patron of Cluny—the king is called "Hildefonsus" in the documents of Cluny[308] and Adefonsus in Spain—would be significant in such a gift. With this destination, it is less surprising that the work of a minor author, little read in France,[309] should be transcribed at Cluny about 1100 in so elaborate a form and illustrated with such magnificence. It is a text that has no place in the liturgy, although in Spain the story of the miraculous appearance to Ildefonsus of the Virgin, seated on his bishop's throne in the cathedral, and her gift of a chasuble, was read in the missals. The other copies of Ildefonsus' treatise from Cluny are bound with texts in praise of the Virgin by Fulbert, Jerome and Odilo, but contain little or no ornament.[310] As an offering of gratitude to the royal Spanish patron of Cluny the unique artistic character of the Parma Codex becomes intelligible.

There was in the choice of this text an additional fitness for a gift from Cluny to Spain, whether to the Spanish king or to the archbishop of Toledo. By including the colophon of Gómez, addressed to Gotiscalc, bishop of Le Puy, and by illustrating the old presentation, the Cluniac donor not only affirmed the antiquity of the friendly relations between the Spanish and French churches evidenced in the writing of a codex of Ildefonsus for a French bishop; the new copy could also be seen as the counterpart in more precious and noble form of an ancient gift from Spain to France. Reproduced so often at Cluny, the manuscript in the Cathedral of Le Puy was surely

303. "Ego Adefonsus rex Leonum . . . mole peccatorum depressus . . . disperatione dejectus, set etiam reatum meorum criminum expavesco . . ."–Bruel, *Recueil des chartes*, IV, no. 3509, pp. 627ff.

304. Bruel, *Recueil des chartes*, no. 3540.

305. Liber de Miraculis, Migne, *Pat. lat.*, CLXXXIX, cols. 904ff., and M. Marrier and A. DuChesne, *Bibliotheca Cluniacensis*, col. 1296a. The promised perpetual tribute was not paid in the 1120's by his grandson, Alfonso VII, and is adduced by C. J. Bishko ("Peter the Venerable's Journey to Spain" in *Petrus Venerabilis 1156-1956*, ed. by G. Constable and J. Kritzeck, pp. 164, 169, 170) as a reason for the abbot Peter's trip to Spain in 1142. At his meeting with Peter in Salamanca, Alfonso paid the arrears and abolished the tribute for good. The abbot's account of the Spanish monk's vision is followed by Peter's explanation that Alfonso was saved from hell because of his gifts to Cluny.

306. For Alfonso's family relations with Hugo and the Burgundian nobility, see Defourneaux, *Les français en Espagne*, p. 22. P. David (*Études historiques sur la Galice et le Portugal du VIe au XIIe siècle*, Lisbon, Paris, 1947, p. 388) thinks that Hugo and the Cluniac monk, Robert, had a major part in arranging the marriage which was condemned at first by the pope as contrary to canon law, since Constance was a fourth cousin of Agnes, Alfonso's deceased first wife.

307. The editors of the catalogue of the exhibition at Rome in 1954 have already conjectured that the manuscript was made for a royal personage (see note 18 above).

308. See Hildebert, Vita Hugonis, Migne, *Pat. lat.*, CLIX, col. 866 (as in the inscriptions of the Parma miniatures).

309. See M. Manitius, *Geschichte der lateinischen Literatur des Mittelalters*, III, pp. 532, 533, 535 for the story of Herman of Tournai's difficulty in finding a copy; he discovered one, finally, in Châlons, which he transcribed for the bishop of Laon. On the other hand, P. Justo de Urbel says of Ildefonsus' treatise on Mary that, apart from liturgical books, the *De Virginitate* is the one most frequently encountered in documents of medieval donations and foundations in Spain. (*Los monjes españoles en la Edad Media*, Madrid, 1933, I, p. 338.)

310. On an illustrated copy from the Cluniac abbey of St.-Martial in Limoges, see Appendix II.

known to Hugo, whose predecessor and friend, the great Odilo, was of Auvergnat origin and had been a dignitary of that cathedral. One of his nephews, Stephen, was bishop of Le Puy.[311]

In considering these possible motives, one must not ignore the importance of the text of Ildefonsus for the religious life of Cluny at that time. It is one of the oldest expressions of the cult of the Virgin, which was then beginning to pervade Christian piety and was especially favored in Cluny. Ascetic in tone, the work of a former monk and abbot who became the chief bishop of Spain, this ancient treatise defending the dogma of Mary's perpetual virginity contained much that was congenial to Cluniac minds. It was also attractive to readers of the Romanesque period because it excerpted the testimonies of the Jewish prophets concerning the birth of Christ—passages which were inscribed on the scrolls of the prophets in Romanesque sculpture and painting and recited in the liturgical drama—the prophet-plays of the Christmas season.[312] The numerous miniatures of the prophets in the Parma Codex exceed the usual requirements of illustration and show how strong was the desire to make visible these ancient foretellers of Christ's coming. The polemic against Jews and heretics in Ildefonsus' book, drawing largely on the prophets and patriarchs of the Old Testament and illustrated in the Parma Codex by pictures of arguing figures, must also have appealed to Christians in 1100, a period when the growth of the towns, of travel and trade, exposed the faithful to the challenge of heretics and unbelievers. At this time arises a new literature of religious dispute: the dialogues with Jews in which passages from the prophets of the Old Testament are cited by Christians as arguments for the Messianic mission of Christ.[313] A few decades later, another abbot of Cluny, Peter the Venerable (1122-1156), in a treatise against the stubbornness of the Jews, addressed them with phrases remarkably like those of Ildefonsus, and appealed, like him, to the testimony of the prophets.[314]

But Ildefonsus had been read and copied in Cluny, as we have seen, by a generation of monks before 1100, and it is possible that the great interest of the Cluniacs in the fortunes of Christian Spain, where they possessed more than twenty houses and had advised the kings ever since the

311. On Odilo's relations to Auvergne, see Mabillon, Elogium Odilonis, Migne, *Pat. lat.*, CXLII, cols. 833, 834.

312. In Cluny the prophets were read regularly throughout the year in the services, according to the Consuetudines of Udalricus (1080's); see Migne, *Pat. lat.*, CXLIX, cols. 643-645, 686. In Cîteaux as well there was apparently great interest in the prophets; it is expressed in the elaborate painting of Christ in glory surrounded by the twelve prophets in the manuscript of Jerome on the Prophets, Dijon, Bibl. mun. 132; Oursel, *La miniature du XIIe siècle*, pl. XLV. The prophets with inscribed scrolls were represented in mural paintings of the late 11th century at Sant'Angelo in Formis and Saint-Savin; earlier examples, perhaps significant for Cluny, are on the bronze doors of S. Paolo f.l.m. in Rome, which were made in Constantinople in 1070, during the rule of the abbot Hildebrand, later Pope Gregory VII and a close friend of Hugo.

On the Ordo Prophetarum of the Christmas liturgy and on the prophet-plays, see Emile Mâle, *L'Art religieux du XIIe siècle en France*, Paris, 1922, pp. 141-147, and Karl Young, *The Drama of the Medieval Church*, Oxford, 1933, II, pp. 125ff.

The taste for the prophets in Romanesque art was perhaps prepared in Ottonian art; the illustrated Reichenau manuscripts give an important place to these Old Testament figures. Cf. Munich lat. 4453, the Gospels of Otto III from Bamberg, s.X ex (Goldschmidt, *German Illumination*, II, pls. 25, 26); Bamberg Cod. Bibl. 76, Commentary on Isaiah, s.X ex (*ibid.*, II, pl. 30); Bibl. 22, Commentary on Daniel, s.X ex (*ibid.*, II, pl. 31). On the silver and ivory cover of the mid-11th century missal of St. Denis (Paris, Bibl. Nat. lat. 9436) busts of ten prophets in squares frame the Crucifixion (Goldschmidt, *Die Elfenbeinskulpturen aus der Zeit der Karolingischen und Sächsischen Kaiser, VIII-XI Jahrhundert*, Berlin, II, 1918, pp. 60, 61, fig. 40, no. 194.

313. On this literature see Margaret Schlauch, "The Allegory of Church and Synagogue," *Speculum*, XIV, 1939, pp. 448-464, and especially pp. 455ff. Also J. de Ghellinck, *L'essor de la littérature latine au XIIe siècle*, Brussels, Paris, 1946, I, pp. 161-167, and Bernhard Blumenkranz, *Juifs et chrétiens dans le monde occidental 430-1096*, Paris, 1960, pp. 67ff., 213ff.

314. See his "Tractatus adversus Iudaeorum inveteratam duritiem," Migne, *Pat. lat.*, CLXXXIX, cols. 507ff.–"Audite ergo, Judaei, et ex scripturis vestris Christum, vel juxta vos Messiam esse agnoscite Filum Dei. Veni ergo imprimis, eximie prophetarum Isaia, . . ." (col. 509); cf. Ildefonsus' repeated use of "Audi" and "veni": "Audi ergo et tu, Helvidi" (Blanco García, *San Ildefonso* pp. 67, 77, 79, 85, 88, 99, etc.). The text of Ildefonsus was perhaps known already in the first half of the 11th century to the abbot Odilo who, in defending the Virginity of Mary against heretics, employs a rhetoric like that of Ildefonsus. Cf. his sermon XIII, on the Birth of Mary (Migne, *Pat. lat.*, CXLII, col. 1029)–"Hanc quam despicis, Manichaee, mater est mea . . . Quid agis, Manichaee? Christi matrem opprimis, non Christum defendis. . . ." In his sermon XII, on the Assumption of Mary, he quotes frequently from the prophets to support his belief in the virgin birth and Christ's Messianic role (*ibid.*, cols. 1024ff.). In the sermons on the Nativity, the Purification of the Virgin and the Incarnation (cols. 999-1004), there is repeated use of "Audivimus" and "videte" as in Ildefonsus' treatise. A text of Ildefonsus could have been brought early in the 11th century not only from Le Puy, but from Spain directly by the Spanish monks at Cluny whose deviant liturgical practice is described by Radulfus Glaber, lib. III, c.3–Migne, Pat. lat., CXLII, col. 651.

first half of the eleventh century, made Ildefonsus an especially important figure. The repeated copying of this old Spanish author at Cluny in the last quarter of the century might in itself be interpreted as a homage to the abbey's greatest patron, king Alfonso of Spain. These manuscripts are the oldest copies of Ildefonsus known to have been written outside of Spain. They are not purely theological texts but also commemorative, for they contain, beside the writings of Ildefonsus, two biographies of the saint which recount his virtues and miracles, though Ildefonsus had no place in the liturgical calendar of Cluny. In the illustration of the Parma Codex, Ildefonsus is more prominent than the Virgin Mary, to whom the central text is devoted.

APPENDIX I

The Contents of the Parma Codex

For the measurements and pagination, see page 7 above.

fol. i–blank.

fol. iv–library numbers and engraved bookplate of the Parma library.

fol. ii–in 18th-century hand: "Quest' opera di S. Ildefonso de Virginitate M. fu scritta da Gomesano Abate dell' Archisterio Ildense nei confini di Pamplona, ad istanza di Godescalco Vescovo Anicense o sia di Le Puy."

fol. iiv–in hand of early 13th century: "Confitemini dn̄o qm̄ bonus qm̄ in sec̄lum" (Psalms 106:1).

fol. 1–old library number "171" and note in Italian that the pages were numbered in 1866.

fol. 1v–full-page painting of the bishop Julian addressing three figures, inscribed IULIAN' EP̄S (Fig. 1); on the upper margin, "171" is inscribed again.

fol. 2–"Iulianus loquitur ep̄s dicens," in gold capitals on a purple ground; in larger capitals on same ground, HILDEFUNSUS MEMORIA, with an ornamented gold initial H (Fig. 32). "171" on upper margin. For the text, which continues "sui temporis clarus . . . ," see Migne, *Pat. lat.* XCVI, col. 43.

fol. 3v–end of Julian's eulogy: "atque in ecclesia beate Leocadie tumulatur, ad pedes sui decessoris, cum quo creditur aeterne frui receptaculo claritatis" (*ibid.*, col. 44).

fol. 4–full-page painting: Ildefonsus at the altar, with two monks and a layman, inscribed HILDEFUNS' (Fig. 2).

fol. 4v–full-page painting: Ildefonsus writing, with four monks at his sides; inscribed HILDEFUNS' (Colorplate 1).

fol. 5–rustic capitals in gold on purple ground: "In nomine dn̄i incipit opusculum prefationis in qua exprimitur humilis devotio; atque pia confessio sequitur," above gold ornamented initial D of D̄S LUMEN VERUM in large capitals. In the D, the bust of the Lord, blessing and holding a raised book in his left hand; below him, the monk Ildefonsus in prayer (Colorplate 1).

fol. 5v–"qui illuminas omnem hominem . . ." (*ibid.*, col. 53).

fol. 9–". . . veritas illa quae deus est, regat salvandum, et in secula seculorum possideat victurum. Amen" (*ibid.*, col. 58). In gold rustic capitals on purple ground: "Hic incipit oratio Hildefunsi toletanae civitatis episcopi ad sanctam Mariam."

fol. 9v–full-page painting: Ildefonsus kneels before enthroned Virgin who holds a book in her raised left hand (Fig. 3).

fol. 10–Large gold ornamented initial D of "Domina mea dominatrix mea . . . filii tui," written in gold Roman and rustic capitals (*ibid.*, col. 58) (Fig. 33).

fol. 12–". . . roborata quid sine amissione teneres" (*ibid.*, col. 59). In gold rustic capitals on purple ground: "Altercatio hildefunsi episcopi contra perfidū Iovinianum."

fol. 12v–full-page painting: Ildefonsus arguing with Iovinianus; each is accompanied by a follower (Fig. 4). Inscription on lower margin "1650."

fol. 13–large ornamented initial A of "Audi tu, percipe tu, Ioviniane; corde sapito," written in Roman and rustic capitals (Fig. 35).

fol. 15–". . . in nodem coaequalem, copulem talem" (*ibid.*, col. 60). At bottom of page, in gold Roman and rustic capitals: "Infidelissimum Helvidium."

fol. 15v–full-page painting: Ildefonsus arguing with Helvidius; inscribed HILDEFUNSUS (Fig. 5).

fol. 16–large ornamented initial A; "Audi ergo, et tu, Helvidi, ad me adtende impudera te . . . me ausculta" (*ibid.*, col. 61), in gold Roman and rustic capitals on purple ground (Fig. 28).

fol. 21v–". . . in hoc momento, in hoc tempore, et in omnia semper secula seculorum. Amen" (*ibid.*, col. 64). In gold Roman and rustic capitals on purple: "Conflictus Hildefunsi Toletanae civitatis episcopi contra infideles Iudaeos."

fol. 22–full-page painting: Ildefonsus arguing with the Jews (Fig. 6).

fol. 22v–large ornamented initial Q of "Qui dicis, Iudee . . . ecce virgo" (*ibid.*, col. 64), in gold on purple (Fig. 30).

fol. 26–half-page painting: Isaiah addressing two Jews. In the text space above, the rubricator has written: "Propheta contra Iudeos." The painting precedes: "Parvulus, inquit, natus est nobis, filius datus est nobis . . ." (Isaiah 9), *ibid.*, col. 66 (Fig. 7).

fol. 26v–half-page painting: enthroned David addressing the Jews. It follows the end of the text of Isaiah: ". . . filius dei datus est nobis. Item David" (Fig. 8).

fol. 27–"Minues eum paulominus a deo" (Psalm 8).

fol. 27v–bust of Isaiah in notched frame. Rubric: "Haec in Isaia." Text: "Virga est ex radice Iesse . . ." (Isaiah 11).

fol. 28–painting on two-thirds of page: Ezechiel and two Jews (Fig. 9). In right margin, in gold minuscules: "Haec in Ezechiele."

fol. 28v–bust of prophet. "Haec in psalmis. Thalamus dei est, quia de utero eius" (Ezechiel 44, Psalm 18, are quoted; *ibid.*, col. 67).

fol. 31–"Item Hieremias." Painting of Jeremiah and two Jews. "Prevaricatione est in me domus Iuda" (Jeremiah 5).

fol. 31v–bust of Isaiah. "Item Isaia. Tota die expandi manus meas . . ." (Isaiah 65) *ibid.*, col. 68.

fol. 32v–half-page painting: Hosea and two Jews. At bottom of fol. 32: "Item in Oseae," in rustic capitals. The painting precedes: "Vae, inquit, eis, quoniam recesserunt a me" (Hosea 7) *ibid.*, col. 69 (Fig. 10).

fol. 36–painting (one-third of page): Malachi and two figures (two-thirds length). Rubric above the painting, in rustic capitals: "Dicit Malachias." The text reads: "Veniet ad templum sanctum suum dominator . . ." (Malachi 3:1) *ibid.*, col. 71 (Fig. 11).

fol. 36v–painting (more than half-page): Christ with cross-staff gives the law, in form of a scroll, to Moses. In upper margin, in rustic capitals: "Item in exodo pater ad legis latorem." The text below: "Ecce mitto angelum meum, qui precedat te . . ." (Exodus 23:20ff.) (Fig. 12).

fol. 37v–half-page painting: Ildefonsus, in monk's robes, with crozier, addresses two figures. "Item, unde venit? . . . Audi ipsum per Salomonem. Ego ex ore altissimi processi . . ." (Eccl. 24) (Fig. 13).

fol. 38–half-page painting: Zachariah addresses two Jews. "Haec dicit dominus deus exercituum. Post gloriam misit me . . ." (Zachariah 2:8) (Fig. 14).

fol. 38v–"Item Isaia." Bust of Isaiah in notched frame, beside text: "Ego sum primus et novissimus. Manus quoque mea fundavit terram . . ." (Isaiah 48:12) (Fig. 29).

fol. 39–painting, two-thirds of page: Jacob blessing his twelve sons. On outer purple border of the page, in reserved white space, is a gold inscription by the rubricator: "Hic benedicit Iacob filios suos." Below the painting: "Item quando xp̄c venit, dicat Iacob in benedictionibus patriarcharum. Non deficiet princeps de Iuda . . ." (Genesis 49) *ibid.*, col. 72 (Fig. 15).

fol. 39v–painting, more than half the page: angel addresses Daniel. In the top margin: "Item in Danihele, ad se loquente angelo" (Fig. 16).

fol. 40–Rubric: "Ubi xp̄s venit, dicat Micheas. Et tu, Betlehem, domus Eufrata" (Micah 5).

fol. 40v–half-page painting: Micah stands before city, addressing the inhabitants. "Item ubi venit, dicat Micheas. Et tu Bethleem domus Eufrata . . ." (Fig. 17).

fol. 41v–bust of Isaiah: rubric: "Isaias." Text: "Item David. Ambulabimus de virtute in virtutem" (Psalm 38). "Item Hieremias in libro Baruch: Hic est deus noster, et non aestimabitur alter ad eum . . ." (3).

fol. 41v–bust of Isaiah: rubric: "Isaias." Text: "Item quare venit, ipse per Isaiam dicit: Spiritus domini super me, propter quod unxit me . . ." (Isaiah 61:1). Below, a painting of Habakkuk (two-thirds figure) beside the bust of Christ, in a medallion over a plant—the fig tree that "shall not blossom," in the text of Habakkuk 3:17 on fol. 42. "Existi in salutem plebis tuae . . ." Rubric: "Item Abbacuch" (Fig. 18).

fol. 42–bust of Zachariah in square frame: "Item quomodo venit, abiectus utique . . ." (Zachariah 9:9). Under rubric: "Item apud Isaiam ex persona dei patris," a painting (less than half-page) of Isaiah and two Jews (Fig. 19).

fol. 42v–"Ecce intelliget puer meus . . ." (Isaiah 52:13).

fol. 44v–full-page painting: Ildefonsus kneels before Christ in Majesty with the four symbols of the evangelists. The text of the vision of Christ in Majesty with the four beasts (Revelations 5:11-13) is not quoted, however, until fol. 90v. In the lower margin the rubricator has written in gold minuscules: "Oratio Hildefunsi ad dn̄m ih̄m xp̄m" (Fig. 21).

fol. 45–ornamented initial A of "Adaperi, ih̄s meus, adaperi os meum" (Migne, *Pat. lat.*, *op.cit.*, col. 74, chap. VI). Below, the rubric: "Hildefunsus contra Iudaeos. Quid egit xp̄s et quia deus sit et homo" (Fig. 22).

fol. 45v–painting, two-thirds of page: Ildefonsus arguing with two Jews (Fig. 20). "Quid egisti, Domine? quantum ad omnipotentiam unitae Trinitatis pertinet. . . ."

fol. 102–end of text of Ildefonsus: ". . . nullum dirimatur ab altero (*ibid.*, col. 104), per numquam finienda secula seculorum. Amen." Painting, two-thirds of page: Gómez writing the copy of Ildefonsus for the bishop Gotiscalc in 951 (Fig. 23).

fol. 102v–full-page painting: Gómez presents the book to bishop Gotiscalc; the book is inscribed LIBRŪ S̄. MARIE (Colorplate II).

fol. 103–"Incipit prologus ad Gotiscalcum episcopum," in rustic capitals in upper margin. Ornamented initial E (Fig. 34) of "Ego quidem Gomesanus" (in Roman and rustic capitals). For the text of the colophon, see page 8 above.

fol. 105–"Transtulit aut̄ hunc libellū scīssimus gotiscalcus ep̄s ex hispania ad aquitaniā, tempore hiemis, diebus ceptis ianuarii m̄sis, currente feliciter aera dcccc. lxxx. viiii, regnante domino nr̄o ih̄u xp̄o, qui cū dō patre et scō spū unus ds̄ gl̄atur in scl̄a scl̄or—amen." In rustic capitals: "In nomine dn̄i nr̄i ihū xp̄i, Incipit vita vel gesta sc̄i Hildefonsi, ep̄i Toletanensis sedis metropolitani, a beato Elladio, ep̄o eiusdem urbis, edita decimo kl̄ Febr̄s."

fol. 105v–ornamented initial E of "Ecce Dapes" (in Roman capitals) "melliflui illius domni Hildefonsi . . ." (*Vita Ildefonsi* by Cixila, here attributed to Elladius; for text, see Migne, *Pat. lat.*, 96 cols. 43-48).

fol. 111–"tegminis quae tibi data est . . . . . . promissa palma victoriae. EXPLICIT" (Fig. 36).

APPENDIX II

The Limoges Ildefonsus

PARIS, BIBL. NAT. LAT. 2833

There is one other illustrated manuscript of Ildefonsus' treatise on the virginity of Mary from this time that is of French origin: Paris, Bibl. Nat. lat. 2833.[315] It contains six drawings at the initials of certain sections of the text:

fol. 1–A seated figure of an ecclesiastic, under an arch, holding the initial E in his raised left hand, and a scroll in his right. The text reads: "Incipit prologus in libro de perpetua virginitate s. mariae. Ego quidem gomesanus . . ." (Fig. 85).

fol. 1v–Two ecclesiastics stand under arches; the left, in bishop's robes, holds a tau in his left and a book in his right hand; the inscription at his feet reads *Gotiscalcus*. Under the right arch a figure raises the initial T in his left hand; on his outer robe, with jeweled borders, the central vertical band, corresponding to an orfrey, is inscribed *Julianus*. The initial T begins the sentence: "Transtulit enim hunc libellum scīssimus Gotiscalcus ep̄s ex hispania ad aquitaniam . . ." (Fig. 86).

Below, on the same page, is a second drawing, of the bishop Ildefonsus enthroned on a folding chair with four lion heads and four beast legs; he has a crozier in his left hand, a raised book in his right. Above the book, in relief against the spring and spandril of the right side of the arch, is the initial H of "Hildefonsus memoria sui temporis . . ." (Fig. 86).

fol. 2v–A large D formed of a curved rinceau with compact acanthus ornament, enclosing a bust of Christ with outstretched blessing hand; below, St. Ildefonsus kneels in prayer. The text follows: "Incipit confessio Hildefonsus (sic) et oracio. Deus lumen verum . . ." (Fig. 87).

fol. 4v–A drawing of the Virgin enthroned frontally with the Christ child in her lap, like a cult image, in an arched niche, with a great star in the upper left;[316] at the left, Ildefonsus in profile prays to the Virgin. There is no initial (unless the star is seen as an O, preceding the text: DN̄A MEA O DN̄ATRIX MEA . . .) (Fig. 88).

fol. 36v–The enthroned Virgin presents a robe to the kneeling Ildefonsus. The inscription reads: "SC̄A MARIA dat vestimentum Ildefonso." There is no initial here, but an incomplete outlined frame. "Ecce dapes melliflui illius domini Hilldefonsi . . ." (Fig. 89).

Although these drawings are very different in style and conception from the pictures in the Parma Codex, we cannot help asking how they are related. The first, of the seated Gómez, and the second (of Gotiscalc and Julian), recall sufficiently the two paintings at the end of the Parma Codex to suggest a possible connection. Is the series here a freely remembered version of the Cluny pictures? The fourth drawing, of Christ in the D with the kneeling bishop praying below, corresponds more closely to the figured initial in the Parma Codex, which illustrates and introduces the same text. The remaining two drawings are unlike anything in our manuscript; but the miraculous offering of the robe to Ildefonsus appears in Madrid Bibl. Nac. 10087. The composition there is so different, however, that we need not consider it further; the common text would be enough to account for the image.

Since Bibl. Nat. 2833 has the colophon of Gómez in front of the text as in Bibl. Nat. 2855 and the correct reading "Albaildense"—unlike all the copies in the Cluniac class—V. Blanco García seems right to suppose that it was copied directly from the manuscript of Le Puy.[317] But the scribe undoubtedly consulted also one or more other versions. He writes *Gomesanus* and *ex Hispania* as in the copies made at Cluny; and he adds the Life of Ildefonsus by Cixila—another feature of the Cluniac group.[318] It is interesting, too, that he has supplied from a Spanish (?) source the final chapters that are missing in the Le Puy Codex and the French copies derived from it. For the connection with manuscripts other than Bibl. Nat. 2855 and the Cluniac group, I note that where Bibl. Nat. 2855 reads "qualiter more" and the Parma Codex (and Madrid 10087) "quanti tremore," Bibl. Nat. 2833 has "quali tremore," a reading found in several early Spanish manuscripts.[319] It is likely that the scribe of Bibl. Nat. 2833 worked from a copy of Bibl. Nat. 2855 which already possessed certain features that had entered the Cluniac family, and from a complete Spanish text.

The correspondence of the drawings on fols. 1 and 1v with fols. 102, 102v of the Parma Codex, and the

315. It is described in Bibliothèque Nationale, *Catalogue des Manuscrits latins*, III, Paris, 1952, p. 132. The dimensions are 235 by 150 mm. In Blanco García's list it is called g_6 (*San Ildefonso*).

316. If it is a star, whether or not it is also the initial O, it has probably been taken from an image of the Adoration of the Magi; a large star, treated as a petaled flower, appears in the Adoration scene in French miniatures of the 11th century from Autun (the troper, Paris, Bibl. de l'Arsenal MS 1169, fol. 13v) and St. Germain-des-Près, Paris (Paris, B.N. lat. 12117; Ph. Lauer, *Les enluminures romanes de la Bibliothèque nationale*, pl. XLVIII), on a capital in the cloister of Moissac, and on the ivory casket from Monte Cassino (ca. 1071-1072) in Farfa (Bloch, *Dumbarton Oaks Papers*, 3, 1946, fig. 251).

317. *San Ildefonso*, p. 38. I note here that in another copy, ignored by Blanco García (B.N. lat. 3781, from Moissac) the Gómez prologue is in front.

318. The life by Cixila is not in the Le Puy manuscript (B.N. lat. 2855).

319. E.g., Toledo Cathedral, MS 35, 7, 9th century. On the variants, see the collation in Blanco García, *San Ildefonso*, p. 136, line 4, who ignores this variant in B.N. lat. 2833.

initial on fol. 2v with Ildefonsus praying to a bust of Christ (Parma, fol. 5), is very striking and makes it difficult to believe that the two sets of miniatures are wholly independent. A connection with Cluny becomes more plausible when we discover that Bibl. Nat. 2833 was produced in a Cluniac abbey, St.-Martial at Limoges. The same hand appears in a drawing of a seated bishop in Paris, Bibl. Nat. lat. 2651, fol. 155—the figure of St. Paulinus, beside the text of Gregory's Dialogues (Fig. 90). This manuscript comes from the library of St.-Martial and contains a list of the abbots of that monastery, written in the thirteenth century.[320] The Ildefonsus text in Bibl. Nat. 2833 is bound with a manuscript of the Occupationes of Odo, abbot of Cluny (fols. 70-126v), which has initials of Limousin style—a B formed of little beasts, an A with interlaced scrolls and animal heads. These two writings of Ildefonsus and Odo were already listed in sequence in a catalogue drawn up by the librarian of Limoges early in the thirteenth century.[321] Their two handwritings correspond to the two scripts in Bibl. Nat. 2651.[322]

If we were certain of the date of Bibl. Nat. 2833, we would be able to reconstruct the relationship with Cluny more easily. But while the manuscript may be dated at the beginning of the twelfth century by script, drawing and style of ornament, we cannot say whether it is older or younger than the Parma Codex. If older, it would permit us to suppose that the Parma Codex was preceded in Cluny by an earlier illustrated Ildefonsus.[323]

320. See the description in the *Catalogue des Manuscrits latins*, under its number.

321. See Paris, B.N. lat. MS 1139: no. 96. Tres Ildefonsi, 97. Odo ad Turpionem. Turpio was the bishop of Limoges at whose request the abbot Odo of Cluny composed his work. In MS lat. 2833 the text begins: "Prefatio domni Odonis abbatis in libro suo quem scripsit Turpioni Lemovicensi epo." In another early catalogue in a Limoges manuscript, B.N. lat. MS 5243, item 67 is Ildefonsos duos (Delisle, *Le cabinet des manuscrits de la Bibliothèque Nationale*, II, p. 494); and in the catalogue drawn up by the librarian Bernard Itier in B.N. lat. MS 1085 in the early 13th century, both texts are listed: 78. "Odo ad Turpionem," 99. "Ildefonsus major," 100. "Ildefonsus minor," 101. "Ildefonsus, ubi sunt orationes domni Anselmi" (Delisle, *op.cit.*, p. 497).

322. Other signs of connection with Limoges: the initial B on fol. 99, with two dogs, in a weakened graphic version of the brilliant H in B.N. lat. 1987, fol. 109, a manuscript of assured Limoges origin. Cf. also the pen-drawn ornament of rinceaux, half-palmettes, etc., in 2833 with the ornament in B.N. lat. MS 743, a Limoges breviary of the late 11th century; note in the latter on fol. 112v the miniature of the Creation of Adam with a beaded capital F in the upper right-hand corner, like the initials of 2833.

323. In the catalogue of the Latin manuscripts of the Bibliothèque Nationale (III, p. 132), MS 2833 is assigned to Spain, 13th century. Perhaps the provincial style of drawing and the horseshoe arch in the drawing on fol. 4v suggested this attribution. The horseshoe form is conceivably an attempt to represent the Spanish world of Ildefonsus; but the horseshoe arch is so common in French art of the 11th century—a heritage from Merovingian and Carolingian art—that it should not by itself influence our judgment on this point. It may be found in other manuscripts of Limoges, in the Cluny Bible, Paris B.N. lat. 15176, fol. 345, and also farther North in manuscripts of Saint-Germain-des-Près in the middle of the 11th century (B.N. lat. 11751, fol. 59). A sign of a non-Spanish origin is the misreading of the distinctively Spanish "era" in the date of the colophon as "erat."

I. INDEX OF MANUSCRIPTS

II. GENERAL INDEX

ILLUSTRATIONS

1. *Bishop Julian*, fol. 1v

2. *Ildefonsus at the altar*, fol. 4

Parma, Bibl. Palatina, MS lat. 1650, ca. 1100

3. *Ildefonsus praying to Mary*, fol. 9v

4. *Ildefonsus arguing with Iovinianus*, fol. 12v

Parma, Bibl. Palatina, MS lat. 1650, ca. 1100

5. *Ildefonsus arguing with Helvidius*, fol. 15v

Ildefonsus arguing with the Jews, fol. 22

Parma, Bibl. Palatina, MS lat. 1650, ca. 1100

7. *Isaiah addressing two Jews*, fol. 26

8. *David addressing the Jews*, fol. 26v

Parma, Bibl. Palatina, MS lat. 1650, ca. 1100

9. *Ezechiel addressing the Jews*, fol. 28

10. *Hosea addressing the Jews*, fol. 32v

Parma, Bibl. Palatina, MS lat. 1650, ca. 1100

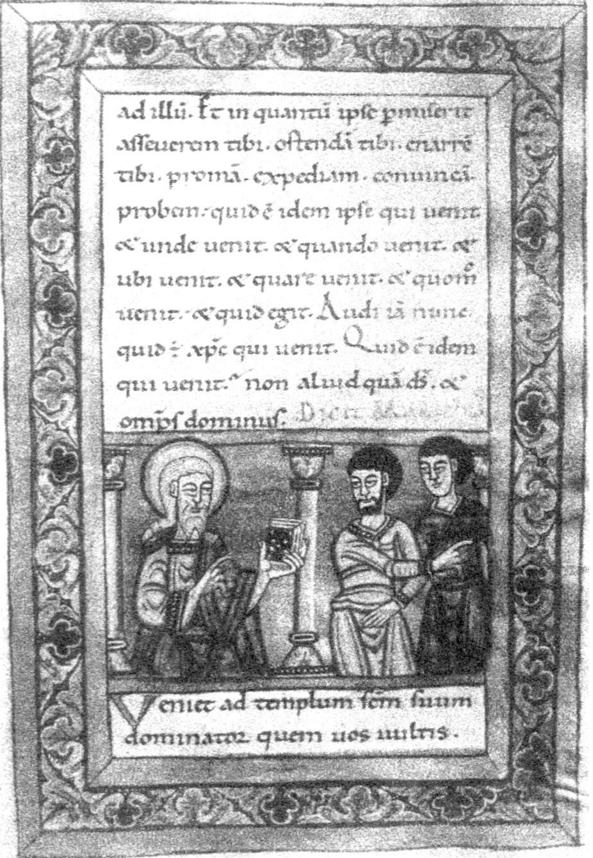

11. *Malachi addressing the Jews*, fol. 36

12. *Christ and Moses*, fol. 36v

Parma, Bibl. Palatina, MS lat. 1650, ca. 1100

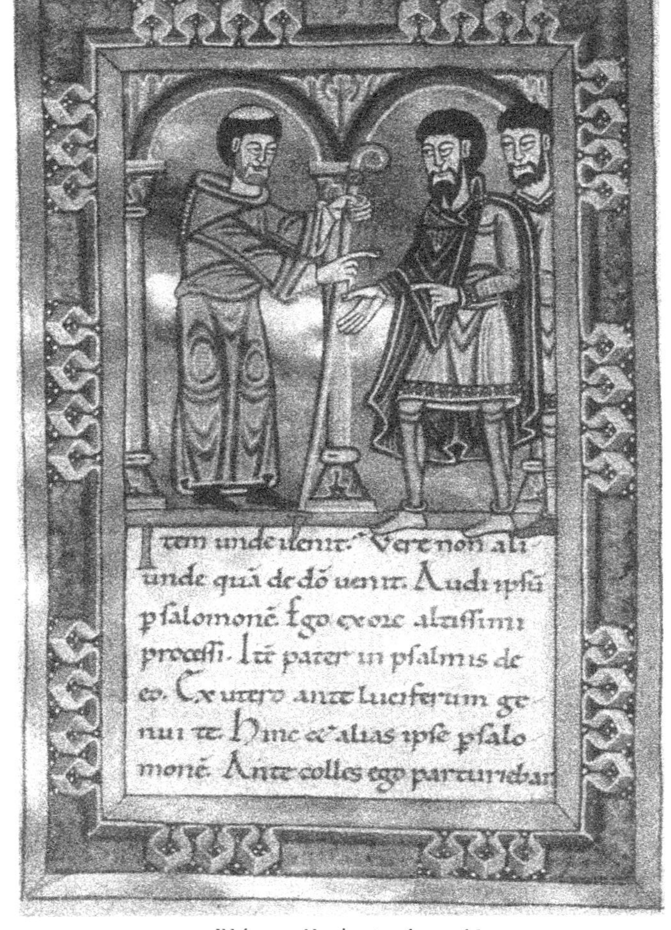

Item unde ilenit. Vere non ali
unde quā de dō uenit. Audi ipsū
psalomonē. Ego ex ore altissimi
processi. Itē pater in psalmis de
eo. Ex utero ante luciferum ge
nui te. Hinc et alias ipse psalo
monē. Ante colles ego parturiebar

Haec dicit dominus ds exercitu
um. Post glām misit me ad gentes
quę spoliauerunt uos. Qui enim
tetigerit uos. tangit pupillam o
culi eius. Quia ecce leuabo manū
meā sup eos. et erunt preda his
qui seruiebant sibi. et scietis quia

13. *Ildefonsus addressing two figures*, fol. 37v

14. *Zachariah addressing the Jews*, fol. 38

Parma, Bibl. Palatina, MS lat. 1650, ca. 1100

15. *Jacob blessing his sons*, fol. 39

16. *Angel addressing Daniel*, fol. 39v

Parma, Bibl. Palatina, MS lat. 1650, ca. 1100

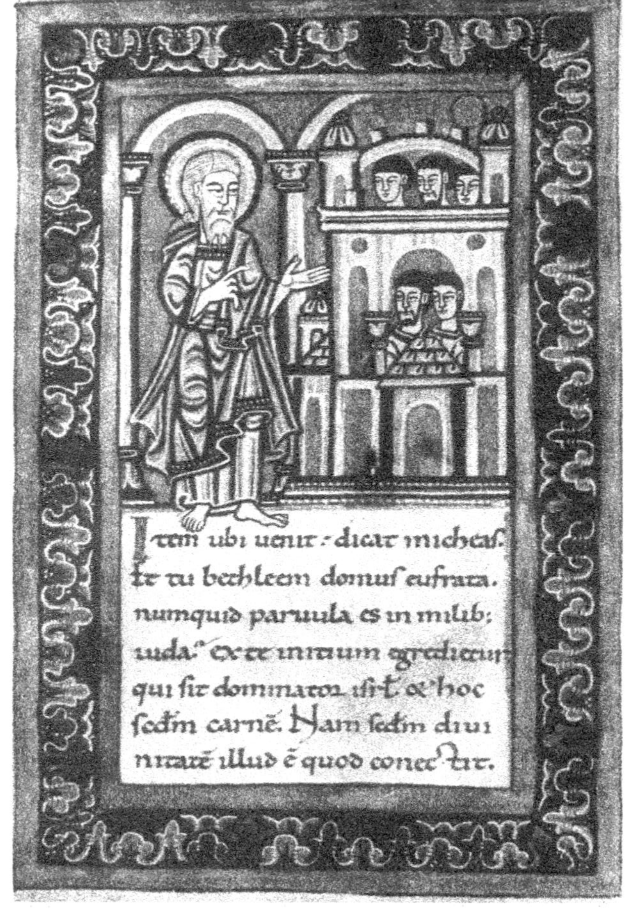

17. *Micah addressing Bethlehem*, fol. 40v

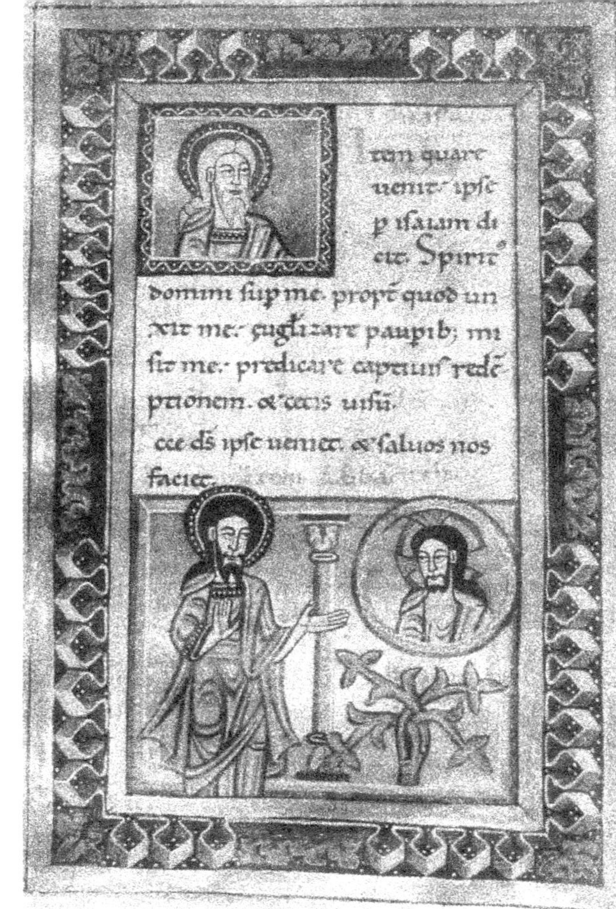

18. *Isaiah* (above); *Habakkuk's prophecy of the Fig-Tree* (below); fol. 41v

Parma, Bibl. Palatina, MS lat. 1650, ca. 1100

19. *Zacharias* (above); *Isaiah and the Jews* (below); fol. 42

20. *Ildefonsus arguing with the Jews*, fol. 45v

Parma, Bibl. Palatina, MS lat. 1650, ca. 1100

21. *Christ in Majesty and Ildefonsus*, fol. 44v

22. *Initial A*, fol. 45 (photo: Pisseri, Parma)

Parma, Bibl. Palatina, MS lat. 1650, ca. 1100

23. *The scribe Gómez*, fol. 102

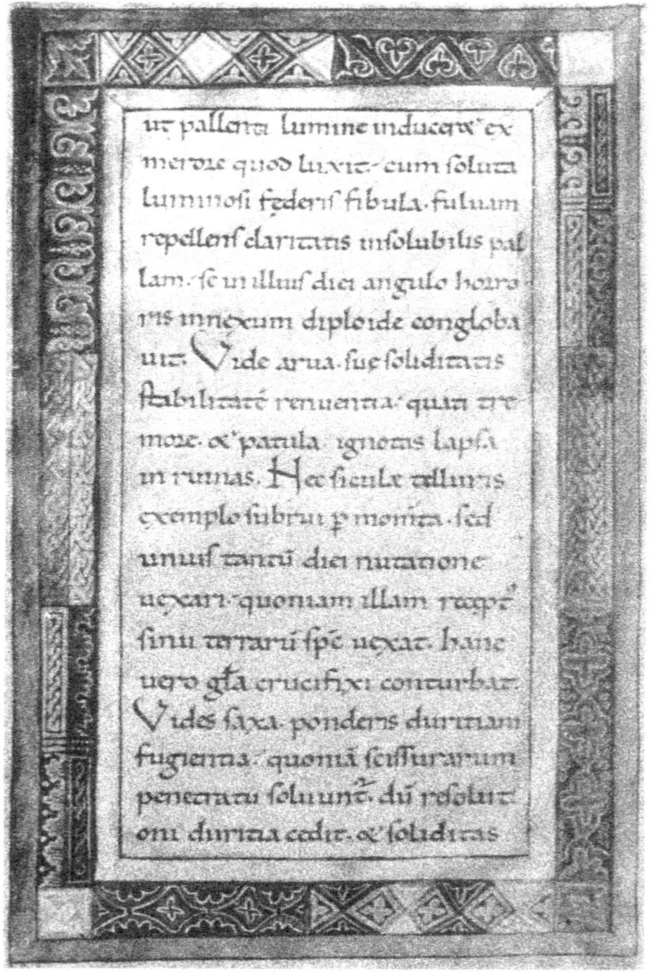

24. *Page of text*, fol. 80v

25. *Ornament of the borders of the text*, Parma, Bibl. Palatina, MS lat. 1650. a: fol. 41; b: fol. 85v; c: fol. 67v; d: fol. 76v; e: fol. 73v; f: fol. 74; g: fol. 68v; h: fol. 77; i: fol. 27; j: fol. 47v; k: fol. 103v; l: fol. 99v; m: fol. 46; n: fol. 24; o: fol. 44; p: fol. 23v; q: fol. 85v; r: fol. 104; s: fol. 18v; t: fol. 24v; u: fol. 109v; v: fol. 109v; w: fol. 108; x: fol. 104v; y: fol. 85v

26. *Ornament of the borders of the text*, Parma, Bibl. Palatina, MS lat. 1650. a: fol. 106v; b: fol. 19v; c: fol. 106v; d: fol. 86; e: fol. 35v; f: fol. 97v; g: fol. 93; h: fol. 96; i: fol. 104v; j: fol. 72v; k: fol. 81; l: fol. 85; m: fol. 75; n: fol. 109; o: fol. 72v; p: fol. 72v; q: fol. 88v; r: fol. 100; s: fol. 81; t: fol. 72v; u: fol. 72v; v: fol. 110; w: fol. 97v; x: fol. 96; y: fol. 97v; z: fol. 85; a′: fol. 101v

27. *Ornament of the borders of the text*, Parma, Bibl. Palatina, MS lat. 1650. a: fol. 91; b: fol. 58v; c: fol. 14; d: fol. 20v; e: fol. 10v; f: fol. 87; g: fol. 94v; h: fol. 59v; i: fol. 107; j: fol. 107; k: fol. 97v; l: fol. 105v; m: fol. 110v; n: fol. 92v; o: fol. 84v; p: fol. 106; q: fol. 90; r: fol. 89v; s: fol. 98; t: fol. 94; u: fol. 56v; v: fol. 104v; w: fol. 85

28. *Initial A*, Parma, Bibl. Palatina, MS lat. 1650, fol. 16, ca. 1100

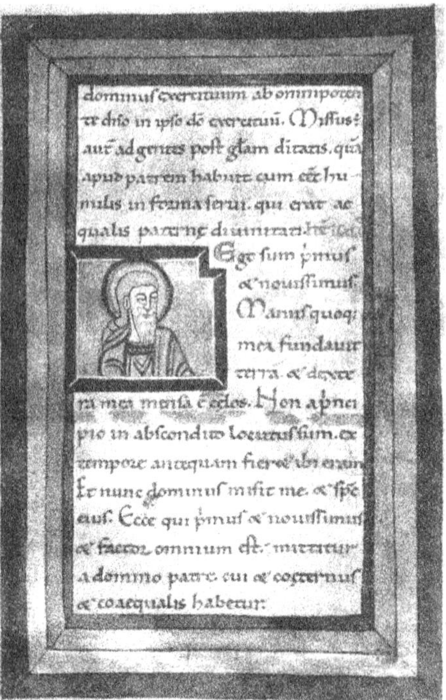

29. *Isaiah*, Parma, Bibl. Palatina, MS lat. 1650, fol. 38v, ca. 1100

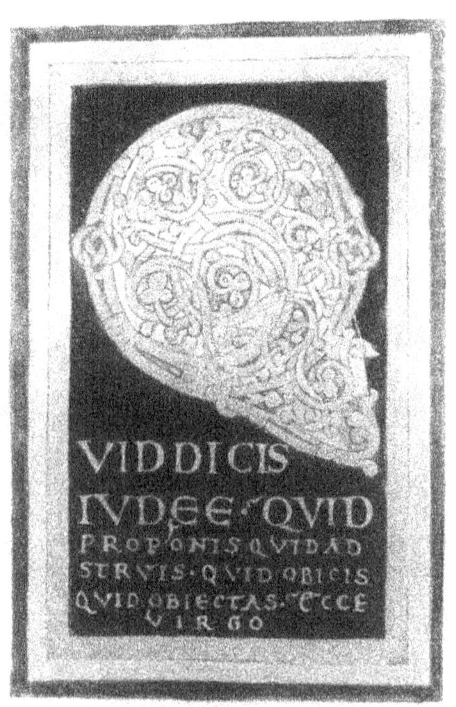

30. *Initial Q*, Parma, Bibl. Palatina, MS lat. 1650, fol. 22v, ca. 1100

31. *Initial Q*, Munich, Staatsbibl. Clm. 18005, fol. 106

32. *Initial H*, fol. 2

33. *Initial D*, fol. 10

34. *Initial E*, fol. 103

35. *Initial A*, fol. 13

Parma, Bibl. Palatina, MS lat. 1650, ca. 1100

36. *Page of text*, Parma, Bibl. Palatina, MS lat. 1650,

37. *Pentecost*, Paris, Bibl. Nat. MS Nouv. Acq. lat. 2246, fol. 79v, toward 1100

38. *Crucifixion*, Paris, Bibl. Nat. MS Nouv. Acq. lat. 2246, fol. 42v, toward 1100 (photo: Archives photographiques)

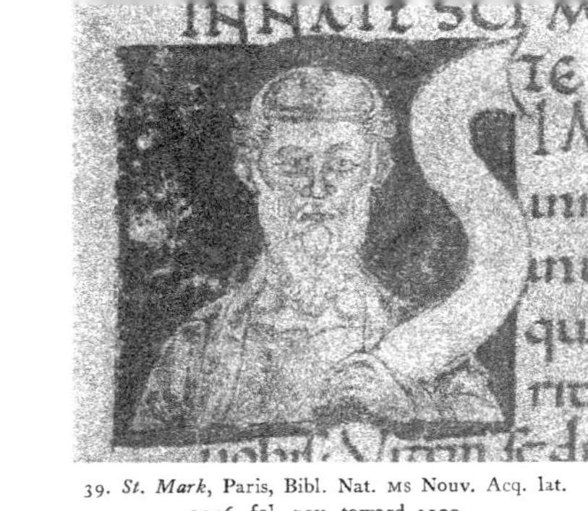

39. *St. Mark*, Paris, Bibl. Nat. MS Nouv. Acq. lat. 2246, fol. 70v, toward 1100

40. *Peter in chains*, Paris, Bibl. Nat. MS lat. 1087, fol. 75 bis, last quarter XI century

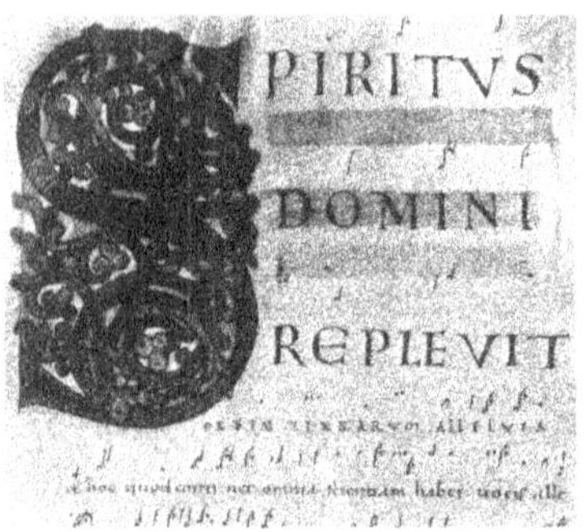

41. *Initial S*, Paris, Bibl. Nat. MS lat. 1087, fol. 70, last quarter XI century

42. Paris, Bibl. Nat. MS Nouv. Acq. lat. 2246, fol. 6

43. *Pen-drawn ornaments*, Paris, Bibl. Nat. MS lat. 1087, fol. 65v, last quarter XI century

44. Apse painting, *Christ in Majesty with Saints and Apostles*, Berzé-la-Ville, ca. 1100 (photo: Archives photographiques)

45. *Christ in Majesty*, *St. Paul and other saints*, apse painting, detail, Berzé-la-Ville, ca. 1100 (photo: Archives photographiques)

46. *Christ in Majesty, St. Peter and other saints*, apse painting, detail, Berzé-la-Ville, ca. 1100 (photo: Archives photographiques)

47. *Abbot or bishop saints*

48. *St. Consortia*

Apse painting, details, Berzé-la-Ville, ca. 1100 (photos: Archives photographiques)

49. *God accepting Abel's sacrifice*, painting of nave vault, Saint-Savin, ca. 1100 (photo: Archives photographiques)

50. *St. Luke*, Montreal, Canada, Collection Mr. Lewis Randall, ca. 1100 (photo: courtesy Mr. Randall)

51. *The Monk John, with Abbot Desiderius, presenting book to St. Benedict*, Monte Cassino MS 99, fol. 3, 1072 (photo: Janine Wettstein)

52. *St. Jerome and Pope Damasus*, fol. 4

53. *St. Jerome and St. Ambrose*, fol. 1, initial F of Frater Ambrosius, Paris, Bibl. Nat. MS lat. 8, vol. 1, end XI century (photos: Archives photographiques)

54. *St. Jerome writing*, initial T, preface to Joshua and Judith, Paris, Bibl. Nat. MS lat. 8, vol. 1, fol. 81, end XI century (photo: Archives photographiques)

55. *St. Martial*, Paris, Bibl. Nat. MS lat. 5296 A, fol. 35, ca. 1100

56. *Abbot Desiderius of Monte Cassino presenting book to St. Benedict*, Vatican MS lat. 1202, fol. 2 (after Inguanez and Avery)

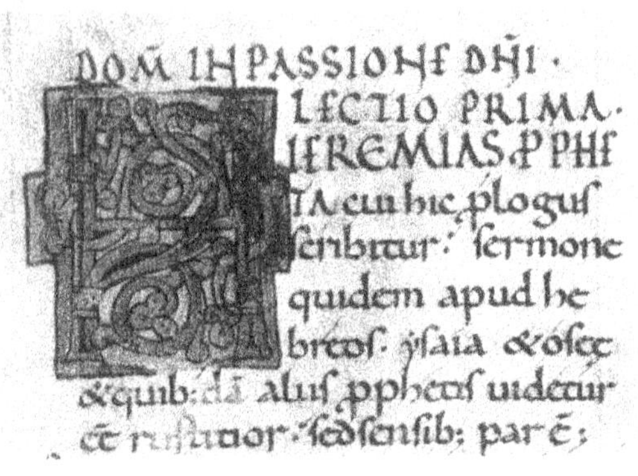

57. *Initial H*, Paris, Bibl. Nat. MS Nouv. Acq. lat. 2246, fol. 36v, end XI century

58. *Initial P*, Paris, Bibl. Nat. MS lat. 1987, fol. 187v, end XI century

59. *Initial P*, Paris, Bibl. Nat. MS Nouv. Acq. lat. 2247, fol. 197v, early XII century

60. *Initials I and C*, Paris, Bibl. Nat. MS Nouv. Acq. lat. 1491, fol. 187v, early XII century

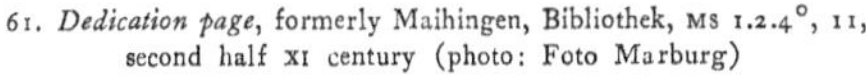

61. *Dedication page*, formerly Maihingen, Bibliothek, MS 1.2.4°, 11, second half XI century (photo: Foto Marburg)

62. *St. Ambrose*, Paris, Bibl. Nat. MS lat. 11624, fol. 22, mid-XI century

63. *Martyrdom of Peter and Paul*, Paris, Bibl. Nat. MS Nouv. Acq. lat. 2390, fol. 32, first half XI century

64. *The Church of the Abbey of Cluny*, from the West Gate, lithograph by Emile Sagot

65. *Initial S*, Paris, Bibl. Nat. MS Nouv. Acq. lat. 1455, fol. 32, third quarter XI century

66. *Initial A*, Paris, Bibl. Nat. MS Nouv. Acq. lat. 1497, fol. 1, end XI century

67. *Pope Gregory and scribe*, St. Gall, Stiftsbibliothek MS 390-391, Antiphonary of Hartker (986-1017) (photo: Zumbuhl, St. Gall)

68. *Otto II receiving homage of the nations*, Chantilly, Musée Condé, leaf of the Registrum Gregorii, end x century (photo: Giraudon, Paris)

69. *Christ*, Paris, Bibl. Nat. MS Nouv. Acq. lat. 1455, fol. 112v, mid-XI century

70. *Ildefonsus leaving his parents for the monastery*, Madrid, Bibl. Naç. MS 10087, fol. 4, ca. 1200 (photo: Moreno)

71. *Ildefonsus receiving the monastic robe*, fol. 4v

72. *Ildefonsus praying to the Virgin*, fol. 9v Madrid, Bibl. Naç. MS 10087, ca. 1200 (photo: Moreno)

73. *Initial D*, fol. 10

74. *Ildefonsus arguing with Iovinianus*, fol. 12v

75. *Ildefonsus arguing with Helvidius*, fol. 16

76. *Ildefonsus arguing with the Jews*, fol. 23
Madrid, Bibl. Naç. MS 10087, ca. 1200 (photo: Moreno)

77. *Angel addressing Ildefonsus*, fol. 100v

78. *Gómez presenting the book to bishop Gotiscalc*, fol. 101

79. *Ildefonsus cutting St. Leocadia's veil*, fol. 109v

80. *Ildefonsus at the altar, followed by king Receswinth*, fol. 110
Madrid, Bibl. Naç. MS 10087, ca. 1200 (photo: Moreno)

81. *Ildefonsus addressing the monks*, fol. 110v

82. *Ildefonsus receiving the robe from the Virgin*, fol. 111

83. *Ildefonsus performing the mass*, fol. 111v

84. *Burial of Ildefonsus*, fol. 112

Madrid, Bibl. Naç. MS 10087, ca. 1200 (photo: Moreno)

85. *The scribe Gómez*, fol. 1

86. Above: *the bishops Gotiscalc and Julian*; below: *Ildefonsus*, fol. 1v

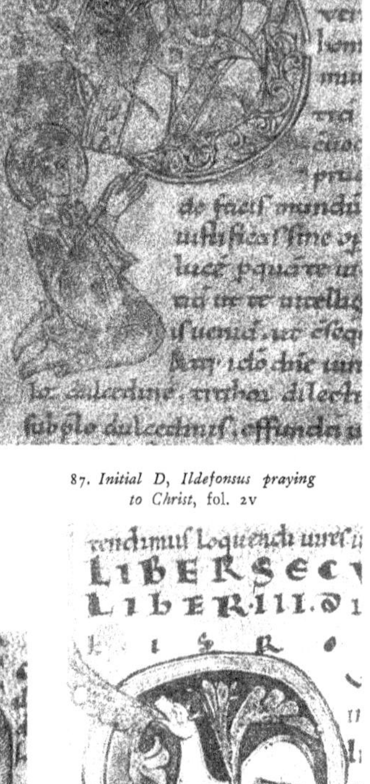

87. *Initial D, Ildefonsus praying to Christ*, fol. 2v

88. *The enthroned Virgin with Christ-child; Ildefonsus*, fol. 4v

89. *The Virgin presenting a robe to Ildefonsus*, fol. 36v

Paris, Bibl. Nat. MS lat. 2833, early XII century

90. *The bishop Paulinus*, Paris, Bibl. Na[t.] MS lat. 2651, fol. 155, early XII century

www.ingramcontent.com/pod-product-compliance
Lightning Source LLC
LaVergne TN
LVHW020636100826
845148LV00012B/2207